TARNISHED CROWNS

ENDORSEMENTS

I've been privileged to write endorsements for many books, but none has given me greater pleasure than to endorse Pam's book *Tarnished Crowns*. Pam builds her story brick upon brick and provides a clear pathway for us to follow as God prepared her for his purpose. It was her vision, birthed through her faithfulness in pursuit of God that created a radical healing movement in the Vineyard. Her pioneering ministry brought her training and experience into the church. More than any other ministry, it dramatically healed and changed my life, saved my marriage, and became key to the health and fruitfulness in the Vineyard Christian Church movement.

Because of the healing my wife and I experienced through Pam's ministry, we were able to share these powerful Biblical principles and practical tools with leaders across the country. Pam encapsulates these principles as she shares her story with dynamic transparency. What you will discover in *Tarnished Crowns* has brought healing, freedom, and wholeness to tens of thousands. I call it "the process of salvation," or the ongoing wholeness that comes as we surrender to God's grace. Pam's brilliantly written and engaging memoir will lift your spirit and give you hope.

Kenn Gulliksen
Founder
Vineyard Christian Fellowship

What I love about Pam's book is the gritty truth about herself and her relationship with God. As she struggles to know God, she realizes faith is not for the faint of heart. She doesn't skirt around the hard issues but goes right through the heart of them to discover God's love. As she has told me, "Christianity isn't a crutch; just the opposite—it's about removing any false dependencies and learning to walk with God." That's Pam's story. Faith develops in the testing ground of life. Don't miss this honest and compelling memoir.

Vanessa Carter
Social Justice Advocate

Tarnished Crowns reads like a Hollywood movie script. It is Pam's adventure as she discovers the life of the rich and famous, only to find that life to be empty and shallow. Her life could have gone like so many thousands who come to Hollywood to fulfill their elusive dreams of being a star but find themselves living a hellish nightmare. But God had different plans in redeeming Pam's dreams. After her transformation, He used her to be a bridge to help those who got caught in the web of horrors that entraps so many. Her former beauty crown has been exchanged for an eternal crown that never tarnishes with beautiful "living" gems. I've had the privilege of knowing Pam personally and seeing how God has used her to be one of His "redemptive" tools in helping thousands.

Judy Radachy
Oasis of Hollywood
Co-Founder & Executive Co-Director

Tarnished Crowns is one of the few books in my lifetime that I read from beginning to end in one sitting. Pam writes with a tone that is at the same time possessed of a blistering honesty about her own life and filled with all the pathos, sensitivity, and sweetness that conveys hope to the hopeless and those struggling with nameless fears and wounds that debilitate them in life. Pam effortlessly blends the depth of her life's experience and her therapeutic training as a marriage and family therapist with a profound, Christ-centered spirituality. She avoids the platitudes of the self-help culture in favor of an emotionally rich vocabulary of recovery and restoration that both young and old will relate to and benefit from. I highly recommend *Tarnished Crowns* to both those foundering in life and those just starting out on life's path in search of meaning and depth in those things that lay ahead.

Russell Walden
Father's Heart Ministry

TARNISHED CROWNS

A Memoir

The Power of Purpose
and Authenticity

Pamela Ann Rice

Notice of Copyright

Cover artwork: Original watercolor by Kenn Gulliksen: "Last Ferry"

Cover design: Agnesam

Interior design: Shauna Perez

Printed in the United States of America
Available from Amazon
First Printing Edition, 2021

DEDICATION

To Charles Jefferson Rice Jr.

My creative and courageous father,
who inspired others to make their dreams come true.

Blessed is the one

who perseveres under trial,

because having stood the test,

that person will receive the

crown of life

that the Lord has promised

to those who love him.

James 1:12

CONTENTS

THE PATH TO TRANSFORMATION

THE BEAUTY OF RESTORATION

ACKNOWLEDGMENTS

For my wonderful Pastor, Kenn Gulliksen, his wife, Joanie, and their four beautiful children who accepted me into their family and revealed God's love.

For my clinical mentors on the Christian Therapy Hospital Program: Dr. Fred Gross, Dr. Lester Nichols and his wife, June, Frank Marklin, and Vi Azvedo. Their integrity and professional commitment taught me how to integrate Biblical principles into sound psychological interventions.

For my precious mother, Helen Rice, the heart of my family.

For my prayer partner, Justin Verdyn, who kept me accountable and prayed me through the roadblocks.

For Vanessa Carter, who showed me the heart of the millennials.

For Russ and Kitty Walden for all ›their love and p›rayer support.

AUTHOR'S NOTE

As a therapist for over three decades, connecting clients with their emotions remains one of my biggest challenges. It is much safer to stay in one's head and try and control the narrative instead of mucking around in the emotional swamplands.

Emotions are complex and mysterious; they are more powerful than thoughts. Emotions can lift us to the heights of happiness or drive us to the pits of despair. They can also compel us to act in shameful ways creating feelings of guilt and insecurity. We often hide our emotions for fear of being judged, criticized, or condemned.

Emotions often dictate our attitudes and drag us around unless we control them. But how can I control what I don't understand? That is why I have elected *not* to pen another self-help book. There are already plenty of good ones out there. Education is vital for growth, but a head full of knowledge will not change me.

It's the *application* of that knowledge that brings transformation. This is where the struggle begins. Change can often be messy, but so is a clogged pipe. To have clean drinking water, the accumulated sediment of resentment, anger, disappointment, guilt, shame, loss, and grief needs to be flushed out, or it becomes stagnant.

It is my desire to share how change happened in my life. I know what a good Christian is *supposed* to look like, but I also know how difficult it is to live up to those expectations. "Man looks at the outward appearance, but the LORD looks at the heart" (1 Samuel 16:7). Real change starts from the inside out.

As a confirmed Lutheran, I knew *about* God, but I didn't *know* him. There's a big difference between *acknowledging* there is a God and *experiencing* him. When I didn't understand his ways, I felt disappointed and reacted like a petulant child. If things didn't work out the way I thought they should, I responded in anger. I believe God understands.

He's not afraid of our emotions. "Be angry but sin not" took me a while to figure out.

Through my honest, transparent *relationship* with him, I learned to trust, and he taught me how to love . . . because he first loved me. Knowing God loved me unconditionally allowed my authentic self to emerge without fear of judgment. It's a liberating experience to enjoy living in this new kind of freedom. Learning to trust an invisible God after heartbreak is not easy. It takes courage to risk opening your heart again once it's been broken.

This journey is the one God designed specifically for me. If God hadn't engaged me the way he did, I might still be like the baby bird stuck in her nest waiting to be fed, never learning to fly. Instead, God grabbed my attention and challenged me to soar above the chaos of living. He stripped away the false pretense my pride manufactured and restored my innocent wonder. Each challenge revealed his faithfulness towards those victimized by life and released a new freedom in mine.

God's overriding hand guided me as I struggled to know him and ultimately learned to love him for the truth of who he is. It is God's desire to make all his children a beautiful reflection of his love as Paul so eloquently expresses in 2 Corinthian 3:2–3, we are God's living epistles that can be easily read and known of all men.

TARNISHED
CROWNS

THE DYING VOICE WITHIN

*For although they knew God, they neither glorified him as God
nor gave thanks to him, but their thinking became futile and their
foolish hearts were darkened.*

Romans 1:21

My stomach knotted with a sudden sense of anxiety. I paused at the top of the stairs. What's wrong with me? I have everything the world considers successful and a life I never dreamed possible—but something's wrong. I tried to shake off the doubt creeping into my well-constructed picture-perfect life.

The limousine arrived to take me to the airport where I'd fly into New York and meet Ed. After he concluded his business meetings, we planned to embark on our European vacation.

Ed and his infectious laughter became an irresistible magnet when we first met. He seduced me with his sophisticated boyish charm, and we soon became a couple. Behind his well-tailored suits, as one of the writers/producers of an acclaimed television show, hid a playful boy I loved but couldn't bring myself to fully trust.

We never made it to Europe. Before our departure, a trust issue raised its ugly head, and we didn't know how to repair the damage.

"Pam, I can't change," Ed said.

"That's not true. What you're saying is, 'I don't want to change.' If you want to change, you can." I didn't understand the truth of what he said. I fought back the tears as his words pierced my heart.

After returning to Los Angeles, our relationship grew more distant, but neither of us dared to talk about the issues. They continued to fester until we agreed to separate. Ed didn't feel like he could change, and I wasn't willing to compromise. My Midwestern values wouldn't let me.

I wanted the fairytale—the one where you get it all—love, commitment, and fidelity. No one taught me anything about the hard work necessary for a healthy relationship. My heart ripped, torn between my love for Ed and what it would cost to compromise my needs. I did that once before, and I couldn't do it again.

Still in my satin bathrobe in the middle of the afternoon, I paced around my lonely apartment before slumping into the kitchen chair. Memories of the betrayals pummeled my brain, crushing my youthful idealism, leaving my soul drained of any joy, hope, or happiness. The vacuum of loneliness numbed my emotions, and I felt dead inside. I'd gotten through broken relationships before. Why can't I get it together now? How did I get here? A thousand condemning thoughts dragged me deeper into my despair.

The weight of the oppression invading my soul didn't frighten me. Disillusionment had swallowed my ability to care. Yet, buried under multiple layers of emotional debris, a faint voice kept crying out, "help."

The thought of going to church crossed my mind, but I didn't see how God could help. I had real-life problems that needed concrete solutions. My issues were emotional, not spiritual. Maybe after I figure things out, I'll reconnect with God.

After seven years in this town, I learned how much Hollywood worships youth and beauty and money. If you don't know the value of your assets or how to use them before they depreciate, game over. Could I be calculating enough to make this corrosive system work before my expiration date? I doubted it.

Curiosity more than ambition caused me to stumble into this world. My insecurities stayed hidden behind a façade to mirror the expectations of those around me. In my naïveté, I loved honestly, never suspecting all the underlying agendas disguised as love.

I grew to hate this town and myself. Powerful men exploit the innocent and beautiful women exchange their charms for more tangible assets—what a deceitful game. Spiritual forces seemed to be at work behind the scene, maneuvering for the soul of every player on this chessboard.

Once I realized the origins of this metaphysical dance, I had to make a choice. Toughen up and play by the world's rules, or find another way.

I lost the will to continue picking up the pieces of my broken heart, haphazardly gluing them together only to have them shattered again. Could anyone restore the mess I made of my life? It didn't seem like there was much to salvage—I would need a new heart transplant, but the kind where there is no human donor list.

IN THE BEGINNING

Chapter Two:
And the Winner Is . . .

UNEXPECTED OUTCOMES

Your eyes saw my substance, being yet unformed.
And in Your book they all were written,
The days fashioned for me,
When as yet there were none of them.

Psalm 139:16 NKJV

"Pam, you have to do this with me," Diane, my childhood friend said as she plopped a brochure for the Miss Racine Pageant on the living room table.

I picked it up for a closer look. "Are you kidding? That's crazy."

"It'll be fun. We can do it together," she countered.

"No way. I'd be too embarrassed." *Where did she get these wild ideas?*

"Are you going to work at the bank all your life?"

"Of course not, we just graduated high school." I tossed the brochure back on the table. "Give me a break. There's plenty of time to figure things out." Diane asked the same question I asked myself. *What am I going to do with my life?*

"Ok, but please just come to the tea before you make up your mind?" Who could resist those pleading brown eyes?

"Alright," I conceded, "but just the tea . . . nothing more." What would people think if I entered a beauty contest? I had thought of being a gym teacher or maybe an airline stewardess, but a beauty pageant contestant?

Miss Racine Pageant Announcement

The number of girls who attended the tea surprised me. They were all dressed in eager anticipation with their well-coiffed hair and Sunday-best dresses. I didn't know any of them except Diane. Mrs. Haberman, the elegant director of the Miss Wisconsin Pageant, spoke about the honor of being chosen to represent our city. I knew I didn't fit their ideal image of a gracious ambassador. As a child, I enjoyed running barefoot through the fields, swinging on the vines in the ravines, and wading along the riverbanks behind our house. I savored freedom. My adventurous nature didn't lend itself to royal behavior or crowns.

I leaned over and whispered to Diane, "Where do they get the confidence to be a queen?"

"It's about scholarships and talent, Pam, not just beauty."

"But I don't have any talent, and I'm not going to college this year, so what am I doing here?"

14

"Shhhh!" Diane seemed irritated with my interruptions.

A middle-aged man, neatly dressed in a bland grey suit, approached our table carrying a camera. "Hello, ladies, would you mind coming with me for a minute?"

We looked at each other and said "sure." He gathered several other girls, lined us up on the balcony outside the meeting room, and took our picture for his article in the local newspaper.

Sure enough, there we were on the front page of the Sunday Society section: "Miss Racine Luncheon Draws Local Beauties." I wanted to die. Diane was thrilled.

Feeling obligated now, I attended the introductory meeting. The pageant director, Mary Lou Hunt, a former Miss Racine, welcomed us. I only went to tell them I had no talent and wasn't qualified to participate.

"Do you sing? Mary Lou said. Before I could answer she continued, "Play an instrument? Read poetry?"

"No." I shrugged. "There's a song I like to pantomime for fun.

"What song?"

"*I'm Just a Girl Who Can't Say No.* The one Ado Annie sings in *Oklahoma.*"

"Show us how it goes," Mary Lou's assistant said.

My parents bought all the records of the musicals they saw in Chicago. I pantomimed the songs to my reflection in front of the big bay window in our living room when they went out at night.

I tried to recite it, but I couldn't remember the words unless I sang them.

"Great. That'll work fine. You can sing it," Mary Lou said.

"No, I can't sing," I protested.

"Pam, it works for the song. You don't have to be a great singer. It's a musical comedy, and you can sell it with your personality."

"Really?" I kicked myself for coming, never imagining it would go this far.

"We'll help you, so don't worry. It'll be great." They made the decision for me, and now I was stuck.

I officially became a participant in the Miss Racine Pageant. Me, the one who thought everyone was better, smarter, and prettier than her. How ironic.

Everyone loves a clown, and that became my self-appointed role. If I made people laugh, they were less likely to say anything bad about me. I concealed my insecurities by being the comedian. I identified with Ado Annie's playful character.

When asked about my picture in the newspaper, I sloughed it off as lunch with my friend. I didn't even tell my mother I had officially entered. If I didn't make it into the finals, I'd be mortified, but if I did, that would be an honor I could live with.

The night of the preliminaries, I told my mom I'd be going to Diane's house, which I did. I just forgot to add where we would be going from there.

When we arrived at the auditorium, several girls came over to reassure me when they saw how nervous I was, "Don't worry, Pam, you'll be fine." Their concern touched me. Despite my playfulness, I did pay attention, and I had an inner determination not to humiliate myself.

When I stepped onto the stage, I took a deep breath and told myself to focus. I followed Mary Lou's directions inside my head, "Shoulders back . . . head high . . . smile!" I reached inside for every ounce of courage I could find to overcome my fears.

Ado Annie's naïve farm girl became delightfully hilarious during the talent portion, and the song landed me in the top twelve.

After the show, I spotted my mother coming down the aisle. She slipped into the audience without telling me. I could never get away with anything.

"Mom! How did you get here?" She came over with a big smile and hugged me.

"I heard you on the phone making plans with Diane." It didn't matter now since I made the finals and hadn't embarrassed myself.

Diane didn't make the cut but generously said, "I am happy for you, Pam. You surprised us all." Even in that awkward moment, my friend embraced my achievement.

"If you hadn't dragged me to that lunch, I'd never be here." I hugged her, "Thank you!"

The next few months became a whirlwind of practices, staging, and public events preparing for the pageant. We visited the Great Lakes Naval Hospital during the height of the Vietnam War. As we stood outside the large hospital ward, I didn't know what to expect. The pungent antiseptic air filled my lungs, and the overcrowded room with damaged bodies jarred my heart. I put on my bravest smile as we entered.

"Hello everybody," said Mrs. Hunt. "These are the finalists for the Miss Racine Pageant." Some of the young men let out a hoot of approval while others whistled.

"Settle down, guys," she said, "Don't get us in trouble with the hospital." Their laughter eased the tension.

One of our girls strummed her guitar and started to sing. The rest of us ambled down the center aisle between the rows of beds, stopping to talk with the wounded soldiers.

"Hi, my name is Pam." I touched the hand of a young man unable to lift his head. "What's yours?"

He turned to look at me and whispered, "James." His eyes were full of pain. He couldn't be more than twenty.

"Where are you from James?" I forced a smile to fight back tears and warmed his cold hand with mine.

"Manitowoc."

"That's up north, isn't it?"

He nodded.

"I've never been, but I'm told it's beautiful."

A faint smile crossed his face.

"I hope you get well soon."

"Thank you for coming." He squeezed my hand before I moved on.

After another girl finished playing a song on the hospital piano, a young man raised the bandaged stubs of his amputated hands and jokingly said, "I used to play the piano before this happened." The smile on his face and his courageous attempt at humor gave the realities of war a tragic face.

The bus ride home took on a somber tone. Silent tears fell. These valiant warriors heroically put their lives on the line for our country's freedom. Now, their futures were robbed from them by the cruelties of war. The memory of their faces and their courage haunted me for years.

The Venetian Theater, one of Racine's beautiful historic landmarks, offered to host the Miss Racine Pageant. The ornate Italian renaissance architecture with its 1,900-seat capacity intimidated all of us.

"Look at that runway," I said, "a plane could take off on that." It jetted out into the audience. "One missed step, and I'll land in someone's lap."

The night of the show arrived. I knew Susan Ruhland would win. In addition to her grandfather owning the bank where I worked; she played beautiful piano and looked the part of the perfect pageant queen: prim, proper, and perfectly manicured.

Since I didn't anticipate winning, the pressure lessened. I didn't like the word "competition." Not competitive by nature, I just wanted to absorb every moment of this exciting new experience.

During the talent portion of the show, my Ado Annie character bounced onto the stage and connected with the audience. She fed off their energy. The chemistry with the audience thrilled her, and the more they laughed, the bolder she became. It gave her a euphoric rush of adrenaline.

I bolted off the stage like a frisky colt thrilled with my performance; now on to navigating the runway in my flowing chiffon evening gown.

After the reigning Miss Racine, Bonnie Bailey, gave her farewell speech, all twelve of us lined up for the announcement of the five finalists and the ultimate winner. Much to my amazement, I heard my name announced.

Wow! I'm a finalist. How great is this? But I still expected Susie Ruhland to win. After the names for fourth, third, and second runner up were announced, the only two left standing on the stage were me and Susie Ruhland.

Then the announcer proclaimed, "First runner up is Susan Ruhland . . . And the winner and next Miss Racine is . . . Pamela Rice!"

The theater erupted in applause. As I congratulated Susie, they came to put a crown on my head and to give me the bouquet of roses.

I was Miss Racine!

What a shocking, unbelievable outcome. I couldn't control my ear-to-ear smile and waved enthusiastically to the audience as they stood to their feet. The roar of their applause thrilled me. They genuinely liked me. Profound gratitude overwhelmed me in this magical moment.

My life changed that night, unlocking an undefined something inside. I found the courage to walk into an unimaginable dream—and came out a winner!

I woke up the next day, like any other day, almost forgetting the night before. When I finally wandered downstairs, the house bustled with energy. Telegrams from city officials along with congratulations from family and friends flooded the kitchen table.

"Good morning," my father said. "Look." He thrust the newspaper into my hands.

Is that my picture on the front page of the Racine Journal Times? So, it wasn't a dream. There, in the living room of our remodeled farmhouse, sat my trophy along with a sparkling crown. I stared in disbelief.

My father couldn't stop grinning or talking about the night. "When you walked out on that stage to sing, I thought, 'Oh, no,' but you were terrific." His excitement tickled me.

"I told you she was good," my mother said. "She did better than at her preliminaries."

I surprised everyone. I'm sure they must have wondered, *How did our scatterbrain little tomboy manage to pull this off?* I completely agreed. How did I?

Mary Lou became my personal chaperone and manager. She devoted herself to my preparations for the state pageant in Oshkosh, Wisconsin. This pageant would be televised statewide with every city sending delegations to support their local queens. Along with the scholarship award, I became the illustrious owner of an elegant white mink stole, a specially designed evening gown, a professional portrait, and gift certificates for outfits and accessories necessary for the state pageant. Every day became like Christmas.

I developed a love affair with my city. They reached into my heart with their kind acceptance and drew the best out of me. In appreciation, I made more appearances than any previous Miss Racine. I loved sharing with the various groups and organizations—from the convalescent homes to the Little League games, from the hospitals to the orphanages. Meeting the diverse citizens of my city was an honor.

A local corporation provided a small private jet to fly us to Oshkosh for the state pageant. Upon arrival, we received our room assignments and the full schedule of events: parades, parties, rehearsals, photo sessions, and sightseeing. Former Miss Wisconsin Sharon Singstock headlined the show along with the reigning queen, Candace Hinz.

Mary Lou had my song professionally arranged for the live orchestra. When I took the stage for the preliminary run-through, I stood dumbfounded, listening to music I couldn't follow and staring at the musicians.

Mary Lou rushed over and said, "What's wrong?"

"I don't know when to come in. Where's the melody line?" They arranged the song for a professional singer, not for someone who wasn't strong enough to carry the melody on their own.

"You can do this, Pam," Mary Lou said. "Just let Ado Annie have fun. She'll sell the song."

The conductor started the introduction again, and I fumbled through the song searching for my notes. I told them I couldn't sing, and now I was about to make a fool of myself in front of thousands of people. Fortunately, Ado Annie's comedic antics outshone any musical mistakes, and I made it through my preliminary performance.

"I told you musical comedy is about personality not voice quality, and you did great," Mary Lou said.

I flopped onto the dressing room couch. "I'm sure glad that's over."

The night arrived for the announcement of the ten finalists, and to my surprise, they called my name. I'd be on live television broadcast throughout the state. And me without a lead melody line!

I used a lavaliere microphone fastened to my costume instead of a hand-held mike. This allowed more flexibility to maneuver around on stage. I managed to get through the song in the preliminaries and had to trust I could do it again—on live television. I tried to shake off my nerves as I paced in the wings. My intro music started, and I stepped into the spotlight singing as I entered stage right:

"It ain't so much a question of not knowin' what to
   do . . ."

I moseyed to the center of the enormous stage, singing and talking to the audience,

"I knowed what's right and wrong since I been ten."

The camera held a close up on my face as I continued,

"I heered a lot of stories an' I reckon they're true
About how girls are put upon by men."

Oh-oh, there's a black hole and empty screen—Pull back! Where did she go?

"I know I mustn't fall into the pit . . ."

There she is. What happened?

I awkwardly picked up my microphone and myself from the floor.

". . . but when I'm with a feller
   I fergit!"

I dusted myself off and stayed in character:

"I'm just a girl who can't say 'no.'
   I'm in a terrible fix!"

The audience cheered as I stepped out of the twisted cord and regained my footing. I held the tiny microphone with my hand as I continued to sing and move around the stage.

"I'm just a fool when lights are low
   I can't be prissy and quaint.

"I ain't the type that can faint
   How can I be what I ain't?

"I can't say no!"

The stage lights blinded me, but when I heard the audience's reassuring laughter, Little Ado Annie's joy returned. She flew around the stage as she snapped into her country girl playfulness. She pranced around pretending nothing had happened. She and I were one, and together we finished the song, belting out the final lyrics in full force and on key.

I ran off the stage to a huge hug from Mary Lou. "You were terrific, Pam. Just amazing."

As I hurried to change for the evening gown competition, the pageant director Ginny Hoberman charged into the dressing room.

"Did you plan that?" she said.

"Are you kidding? I tripped on the microphone cord."

"Well, that was pretty brilliantly timed," she nodded then quickly disappeared.

Mary Lou and I glanced at each other and burst out laughing.

Pam performing Ado Annie—after the fall

I hurried onto the stage for the final number and the top-five announcement. Much to my amazement they called my name as a finalist. I stepped to the microphone to answer one last question from the judges: "Who do you admire most and why?"

I chose Walt Disney. "His creative imagination inspired many and he designed a wonderful world that made people smile. The happiness he brought into this time of unrest is admirable." The audience applauded in approval as I returned to my seat, relieved that something came out of my mouth.

We lined up for the announcement of the new Miss Wisconsin. It's hard to explain the energy bouncing off every person in that room. The intensity in the air was magnetic and the tension palpable. I far exceeded my limited expectations. I felt the people who supported me surrounding me in spirit as I awaited the announcement.

Candace Gail Hinz shared her final words then stepped down to prepare for the new reigning queen. The announcer stepped back to the microphone and shared the judges' results:

"Fourth runner up is . . . Miss Racine, Pamela Rice!"

Stunned in disbelief, I rose to accept the huge trophy. What an honor. All I remember is Barbara Burke Baugh, Miss Milwaukee, won the crown for Miss Wisconsin and went on to become second runner-up to Miss America.

Terry Meeuwsen, Miss Green Bay, also a runner-up, later reentered the pageant, became Miss Wisconsin, and won Miss America in 1973. She went on to co-host the *700 Club*, a Christian television talk show. Being among these talented and distinguished women made bringing this additional honor home to Racine even more significant to me.

The honor of being Miss Racine caused me to search for ways to express my appreciation for my city. Being embraced by their love both humbled and encouraged me, and their acceptance caused me to believe in myself.

This experience redefined my life in unexpected ways. It became a rite of passage for me. By pressing through my fears and overcoming my insecurities, I uncovered unique abilities that surprised me. There was more to me than I realized. Who knew I could step on a stage in front of hundreds of people and talk or sing or make people laugh? Who knew I had anything of value to say that people might want to hear?

In this season of growth, I found courage, strength, and resilience I never knew I had. I wondered what other discoveries I might find as I continued to challenge my limitations and self-imposed boundaries.

Eighteen-year-old Miss Racine

24

Chapter Three:
Disillusioned Daze

LIFE IS NOT WHAT I EXPECTED

If any of you lacks wisdom, let him ask of God, who gives to all liberally and without reproach, and it will be given to him.

James 1:5 NKJV

I spent a year as Miss Racine, and now I had to consider what to do next. I enjoyed the performing arts and flirted with the possibility of musical comedy. Posing for photo sessions and advertisements made me consider modeling. Giving up my crown and stepping back into a normal life did not appeal to me. I had reached the pinnacle of success for a young girl in my hometown. If I wanted to continue challenging my growth with new experiences, I needed to look beyond the borders of Racine.

Scouring the Sunday *Chicago Times* job section, I came across an ad for an executive secretary. I lined up an appointment, hopped on the train, and interviewed with the employment agency. They hired me as an executive receptionist. They also directed me to a nearby rooming house for women with access to the shared kitchen. Not the best accommodation, but for twenty-five dollars a week, I couldn't complain.

My undaunted enthusiasm reminded me of the aspiring young actress, Ann Marie, from the hit TV series *That Girl*. Marlo Thomas played the lead actress who left her hometown of Brewster, New York, for the bright lights of New York City. She set out to pursue her independence and live out her creative dreams, much to the concern of her family. I could relate.

My current world revolved around my pageant family where I maintained the center of attention. I still wore those rose-colored glasses in my expectations of Chicago. Why wouldn't Chicago embrace me the same way Racine had? Dreams for the future overshadowed the starker realities in front of me. The door to this exciting new adventure opened, but I worried how my parents would react. On the train ride home, I rehearsed various scenarios on how I could respond to their objections.

I rushed into the house just in time for supper and announced, "I got a job today. . ." Now comes the tricky part, "in Chicago." I blurted it out and hoped for the best.

"Chicago?" my mother said. "When did you go to Chicago?" My mother's world could fit on a postage stamp, and she would never think of taking a train to Chicago alone.

"Today. Bell Savings and Loan hired me, and I start work Monday."

"Monday?" she said as she stopped scooping the potatoes into the bowl.

"I even have a place to stay." I pulled my chair out and sat at the table. "Can you and Dad drive me down Sunday?"

"I'm not sure how your father will feel about this, Pam." I sensed the warning in her voice.

My father managed the meat department at the grocery store on Monument Square downtown. At night he would cut steaks for a trendy restaurant to earn extra money. He also built our first home after I was born. There wasn't anything my father couldn't do. He worked hard and took pride in providing for his family.

I didn't look forward to that conversation. I reminded myself I finished high school, turned nineteen, and interacted with an entire city full of diverse people. I am an adult. Chicago would be a baby step into the larger world outside my door. I'd be far enough away to be on my own, yet close enough that, if I ran into trouble, I could be home in an hour.

The weight of my father's steps on the stairs caused a tinge of anxiety.

"Your mother tells me you got a job in Chicago?" My dad, still in his white work shirt, stood in the doorway to my bedroom. "What made you decide on Chicago?" His brow knit with concern. "It's not the safest city."

"It's not that bad." My comment didn't seem to convince him.

"You can have any job here in Racine or even Milwaukee, but Chicago?" He shifted his weight and leaned his hand against the doorjamb.

"It's a good job, and there are lots of opportunities there."

He issued a litany of hypothetical scenarios to discourage me until I finally said, "Dad, if it doesn't work out, I'll come home. You and Mom can come down and visit me. It's not that far."

One of nine children born during the depression, my father joined the air force at seventeen during World War II. He had his own dreams of seeing the world, so despite his reluctance, he said, "I guess you've made up your mind. I can't stop you, but you'd better call if you need anything." As much as he wanted to protect me, I believe he understood.

I didn't like disappointing my father, but I couldn't stay. I finished packing, and on Sunday we drove down to Chicago while my father continued to point out the typical list of dos and don'ts for living alone.

My mother assumed a brave face as she stepped into the dimly lit, dingy rooming house. We passed the community kitchen with individual locks on the cupboard doors and made our way to my small, sparsely decorated room. I hoped she wouldn't notice the hole in the wall behind the frayed chair in the corner or the drip in the sink across from the bed. Her eyes reflected concern as she glanced at my father.

"Pamela, are you sure you want to do this?"

"It'll be okay, Mom. This is just a temporary place until I figure things out and can afford a place of my own."

My father deposited my suitcase on the bed and set the bag of fruit on the table next to it. He reached into his pocket and handed me two twenty-dollar bills.

"If you need anything—and I mean, anything—you call us. Promise?"

"Thanks, Dad, I promise. I'll call you tomorrow."

We hugged goodbye, and I watched them drive away. It took courage for them to leave me there that day. I loved them for supporting my decision despite their concerns.

The excitement of being on my own for the first time outweighed any worries I had about my dubious surroundings. My idealism made me feel immortal and gave me courage born of ignorance. At nineteen, I had boundless energy, a heart full of optimism, and limitless possibilities.

Chicago. . . What would life be like in this strange city? I settled into my room and dreamed of future successes. I wanted to conquer the world and do something exciting with my life. I wasn't sure what that would be yet, but I'd figure it out.

I took my seat across from the elevator at the desk with its extra-large bowl of candy. There were only three desks on the executive floor: those of two executive secretaries to the president and vice president and mine. The executive secretaries took pride in their prestigious positions and were too busy attending to their bosses in the offices behind them— and too far away—to engage in friendly conversation. I didn't like being ignored and thought maybe I did something to offend them. The quiet floor became lonely with little to do except pick at the candy and wait for the elevator doors to open.

I expected life in Chicago to be more exciting, but my job did not live up to those expectations. The daily routine started to grow monotonous. Fortunately, there were occasional surprises that broke up the boredom.

The downtown bus stopped across from my rooming house. One morning the door opened, and the heavyset male bus driver greeted me with a song. "Good morning, pretty lady. Isn't it a glorious day? Come on in and enjoy the ride as I take you on your way." *Are you kidding me?*

Everyone laughed as this jovial bus driver, with his broad smile and lighthearted attitude, persisted in singing to every unsuspecting passenger who stepped on his bus entertaining his captive audience. These unpredictable moments delighted me most about Chicago.

During rush hour, the city became a madhouse. Everyone hurried to catch the "L" trains or buses, pushing and shoving their way through the crowded streets. Stepping onto a bus packed wall-to-wall with people, one could hardly breathe. One day when I was stuck in the back of one on my way home, I noticed a friend step on board. I waved at her through the layers of people, but she ignored me. I tapped the shoulder of the man standing in front of me, "Excuse me, sir. Do you see that girl in the plaid coat with blond hair?"

He strained to see her, "I think so."

"She's my friend. Could you help me let her know I'm on the bus?" He smiled and tapped the girl in front of him and pointed out my friend. She did the same to the person in front of her. Everyone watched in amusement. This process continued throughout the crowded bus. The last person tapped my friend and pointed her back to the waving idiot in the rear of the bus. Everyone but my friend burst into laughter. At least it made the ride home more enjoyable.

Little by little, almost imperceptibly, I grew disenchanted with life. The humdrum tedium of working nine to five day after day began to wear me down. Chicago didn't welcome me the way I thought it would, and people were not as friendly as I anticipated, except for the rare exceptions like my singing bus driver. Was there something wrong with me? I didn't seem to measure up to an undefined standard of behavior. As a result, my confidence soon began to dwindle, and my enthusiasm deteriorated.

I grew so misanthropic that when I took my seat on the bus, I'd sit in the middle, hoping no one would sit next to me.

"Is this seat taken?" a man asked.

"No." I exhaled a sigh of disgust, moved over, and glared out the window.

He didn't deserve my disdain. My attitude made me appalled with myself more than anything else.

When people got off the elevator at work and saw the big bowl of candy, they politely asked, "May I have one?"

"Of course," I said, while inside I barked, *What do you think it's there for?*

I despised this growing irritability. I didn't understand my reactions, but I knew I wanted more than the boredom of sitting at a desk.

The gloominess of the rooming house lost its fascination and I decided to move. I had befriended a bank teller who worked downstairs in my building, and we decided to rent a one-bedroom apartment in a high-rise on the north side. The apartment's enormous picture window with its breathtaking view of Belmont Harbor clinched the deal.

Every night, as I tried to fall asleep, I reviewed the day, analyzing every conversation and interaction. I nitpicked what I could have or should have said and beat myself up unjustifiably. I've always been my worst critic.

Late one afternoon, home alone, I sat on the couch watching the tiny speckled boats floating in Belmont Harbor. The billowy clouds drifted by tempting me to climb aboard and sail away. Then, something extraordinary happened. God tipped over his heavenly inkwell, and the dark ink of night oozed across the bright sunlit sky, quietly devouring it. The day smiled bravely as this meandering darkness gently kissed her goodnight and covered her with a blanket of freshly lit street lamps and twinkling headlights. Darkness had consumed the city. This fascinating poetry in motion mesmerized me but also symbolized the growing darkness creeping into my soul.

I grabbed my coat and headed to the roof. The brisk Chicago wind whipped my face and bit into me as I leaned over the edge of the building.

"What are you doing to me?" I shouted at the city as if it could hear me.

Life paid no attention to the girl on the roof.

"What did I do to you?"

I released my tirade on the city, but the brutal wind swept my words into the night, silencing my pain. My cold hand brushed the tears from my face as the anger burst forth.

"Why is there so much confusion?"

After condemning the city for its unfairness, I turned my face to the night sky.

"And you! Where are you?" I ranted at God. "Life is not supposed to be like this. We're supposed to be a family and love each other." That's all I remembered about God from Sunday school.

I slid down the wall of the corner I had backed myself into and buried my head in my knees. Disillusioned with life, I cried harder than I had in a long time.

How do you prepare someone for life? Where do you learn the skills to handle conflicts, emotions, people? I didn't have a clue how to navigate the day-to-day, often tedious, realities of real life without my former crown.

My crown had been a ticket to love and acceptance, but now I had to learn to live without it. Reality slapped me in the face, and I smarted from its sting. With my rose-colored glasses shattered, I encountered the cold, sinister side of life that pummels the idealism of innocent young dreamers.

My anger subsided as a strange calmness settled over me and the piercing wind forced me up. Unleashing my pent-up emotions left me drained but peaceful. I examined the city through that stillness.

A scenario popped into my head: If a man has trouble with his wife and they have a fight before he leaves for work, he brings his frustrations to work. When he walks into the office and his sweet secretary says, "Good morning," he may grumble at her and demand, "Where is my coffee?" She thinks he's upset with her, when it has nothing to do with her but things she knows nothing about.

Life is a chain reaction of cause and effect. *If I take things personally, I'll become defensive and miss the deeper issues. It's not always about me.* That profound thought made sense and gave me insight that brought comfort. For the first time in weeks, I had a good night's sleep.

Not long after that, I left Bell Savings and Loan for Arkham Artist and Dunwich Productions, a small music management company in Old Town. Producers Bill Traut and Bob Monaco handled the Cryan' Shames, Minnie Ripperton of the Rotary Connection, and the American Breed, whose single *Bend Me, Shape Me* was climbing the charts.

Working at the management company provided both wonderfully crazy people and unpredictable challenges. Music flooded our offices, a drastic change from the reserved tomb of enforced silence at my previous employment.

The late sixties proved a fascinating time in Chicago, and Old Town embodied the center of that creativity. I joined an experimental music workshop conducted by Bill Russo located in a small theater down the street from The Second City, an improvisation group where comedians like Amy Poehler, Tina Fey and Stephen Colbert began their careers. I came alive in this creative environment.

In 1968, Chicago held the Democratic National Convention during the height of the Vietnam War protests. Abbie Hoffman and Jerry Rubin cofounded the Youth International Party known as the Yippies. They staged ongoing protests throughout the city, threatened to put LSD in the city's drinking water, and nominated a 200-pound pig for president. Lincoln Park, not far from Old Town, became their campground.

The city flooded with thousands of protesters, from the Black Panther party to communists and revolutionaries to flower children and anti-war peaceniks. Mayor Daley deployed 12,000 police and 5,600 national guardsmen, and another 5,000 regular army soldiers to disband their activities. Earlier in the year,[1] during the riots following the assassination of Rev. Martin Luther King Jr., the mayor had ordered police to "shoot to maim or cripple anyone looting." In the wake of that sentiment, bringing in such a heavy hand made the protests worse. Horrific violence broke out with beatings and tear gas. The conflict played out on live television in front of the country. It horrified me to see these young activists beaten by police in riot gear.

When I entered the theater for rehearsal, I found strange people rushing around. *What's going on?* I peered downstairs and saw the basement full of Yippies who escaped the conflict. The battered, bruised, and disheveled Yippies sought refuge in our theater and turned the basement into a makeshift infirmary.

Abbie Hoffman, an influential, charismatic anarchist, came in with his fiery rhetoric. I understood his appeal and ability to stir passion in the hearts of his followers. What I didn't understand was what the political and social activism hoped to accomplish. No one supported the war in Vietnam or trusted Daley's police. Everyone knew Mayor Daley and his corrupt politicians ran the city, and no one liked the Yippies.

Jerry Rubin summed it up[2], "We were dirty, smelly, grimy, foul, loud, dope-crazed, hell-bent and leather-jacketed. We were a public display of filth and shabbiness, living in-the-flesh rejects of middle-class standards."

I wanted to pummel the police, shake the Yippies, and scream, "What are you doing?" It didn't make sense to me. Ironically, Rubin ended up working on Wall Street of all places.

This became a war of generations—the establishment versus the anti-establishment—a fight for freedom of expression and breaking limitations. But was it worth the young lives that were beaten, stomped on, and bloodied? I never considered myself an activist, although I understood their fight. But violence didn't help anyone.

These challenging experiences were more than I bargained for— Chicago in the sixties held no resemblance to my quiet, safe Racine. The sexual revolution burst into full swing along with all the other revolutions. Life was itching to break out of its Victorian shell of *Leave It to Beaver* and *Father Knows Best*. Everyone wanted to know *who* knew best, and they thought they could find it in their sexual liberation, hallucinogens, political anarchy, or rock and roll. The Beatles wanted to hold my hand, and Bob Dylan wanted everyone to get stoned.

I understood the unrest but considered myself more an observer than an activist. Nevertheless, something compelled me to keep pressing on to find where I belonged. I passed through these revolutions exploding all around me and kept searching.

Once the Democratic Convention left town, Chicago slowly returned to normal. I signed with a modeling agency that began sending me out on auditions. Many major trade shows held their conventions at the Navy Pier, making it a lucrative place to start modeling. Opportunities picked up, and I quit my job at the management company to pursue modeling full-time. My boyfriend, Sam, a music agent I met through work, received an offer from a famous talent agency in California.

"Come with me, Pam," he pleaded. "We'll make it a vacation. We'll drive cross-country, and you can fly back in a week or two." It sounded like fun, and my roommate just left to get married, so I said, "Ok, why not?"

I had traveled the East Coast on a family vacation and looked forward to exploring more of the country. Every state has unique qualities that set them apart; the landscape, dialect, dress, and attitudes intrigued me. I'd pick up modeling when I returned home.

We arrived in California, and as we drove down Sunset Boulevard, a jolt of electricity shot down my spine. Giant billboards lined both sides of the street with pictures of famous music groups, blockbuster movies, and Las Vegas headliners. This magical atmosphere stimulated my senses.

As we drove past the Whiskey À-Go-Go where famous bands showcased, I wondered how a street could create this much excitement. Finally, I entered the Land of Oz, and my name wasn't Dorothy. *This is where I have to stay. This is where I'll grow.* My feet hadn't touched the ground before I knew I'd reached my destination.

I called my landlord and asked her to sublet my apartment then called my mother.

"Mom, can you and Dad pack up my apartment and bring my stuff home?"

"What are you talking about?" Her voice expressed alarm.

"I've sublet my apartment and decided to stay in Los Angeles." I could feel the disappointment in her silence. "Don't worry; it's going to be alright."

My short holiday turned into a whole new chapter in my life.

Chapter Four:
When Things Unravel

HELPLESS TO HELP

Above all, love each other deeply,
because love covers over a multitude of sins.

1 Peter 4:8

Sam introduced me to Patty Duke, the Oscar-winning actress of *The Miracle Worker* and star of *The Patty Duke Show*. She became my first friend in the city.

"You're welcome to stay with me," Patty said, "Until you get on your feet."

"Are you sure? I don't want to inconvenience you." Her kindness touched me.

"Not at all. Since you and Sam broke up, don't you need a place to stay?"

I did, but I never considered her place. Sam's new job kept him on the road with the groups he represented and made our relationship impossible. I accepted her generous offer and moved my suitcase into Patty's luxury apartment overlooking Sunset Boulevard.

Patty was dating Desi Arnaz Jr., the son of Lucille Ball and Desi Arnaz of the *I Love Lucy* TV Show. They introduced me to Desi's close friend Tony Martin Jr., the son of singer Tony Martin and the beautiful dancer/actress Cyd Charisse. Tony and Desi kept Patty and me entertained with their adolescent humor and shenanigans.

"My parents want to meet you," Tony said. "We're invited for dinner."

The prospect of meeting his parents unnerved me as we pulled into the driveway of his sprawling Beverly Hills home. Tony Sr., a fine-looking man with thick dark hair, greeted us with his elegant charm. He hugged his son and ushered us into the palatial living room.

"Hi, Mom," Tony said. "This is Pam." Tony's stunning mother floated into the room with the graciousness of a regal queen. She embodied all the Hollywood glamour I'd read about. I didn't know if I should curtsy or kiss her hand.

"It's a pleasure to meet you, Pam." She embraced me with a smile and gestured us into the dining room.

The table, with its flower arrangements, gleaming silverware, and numerous stemware selections, matched the elegance of their queen. Never having dined with Hollywood royalty, I didn't know what silverware to use first. Afraid of making a mistake, I followed their lead and hoped they wouldn't notice my self-consciousness.

The house staff served us while everyone casually conversed . . . just dinner at home with the folks! I liked the sweetness between Tony and his parents. The candles flickered, and the dream dinner concluded with a scoop of Italian sorbet. I made it through the evening, relieved I had no major mishaps.

There wasn't much emotional difference between Desi at seventeen and Patty at twenty-three. Desi had maturity beyond his years, and Patty had a wonderful childlike playfulness. They seemed to genuinely love each other. Tony and I were thrown together so we could hang out with them but never developed anything more than a friendship.

I curled up on Patty's living room couch, about to leaf through a new magazine when she came out of the bedroom and said, "*My Sweet Charlie* is being screened tonight. Let's go."

"Great!" Delighted to see her new made-for-TV movie, we quickly jumped into her Mercedes and headed to the studio.

We slipped in late and sat huddled in the rear of the screening room as the movie began. "I don't want anyone to know I'm here," she said.

My eyes kept darting from the larger-than-life Patty I saw on the screen to the diminutive Patty scrunched in the chair next to me. The creative transformation from reality to her on-screen character stunned me.

And just as quickly as we slipped in, we disappeared. Patty won an Emmy for her powerful performance as a southern white girl disowned by her family after becoming pregnant. She hides in an abandoned lighthouse, and Al Freeman Jr. plays a black attorney falsely accused of murder who decides to hide there as well. Both gave powerful performances in this racially charged depiction of Southern culture in the 70s.

Patty generously arranged for us to have dinner at the Factory, a private club in Hollywood. After several glasses of wine, she shared about her abusive childhood. It disturbed me to learn how her managers exploited her as a child, and I lost track of my wine consumption. On our way home, Patty stopped for gas and stared at me. "Pam, are you going to be sick?"

"No," I said, then immediately turned to the rolled-up window and expelled my expensive dinner. I rushed to the restroom while Patty and the gas station attendant cleaned the car. She could have disowned me as her friend, but she never spoke a word of reproof.

"It's ok," she said and helped me back into the car.

"Patty, I'm so sorry . . . I'll clean everything tomorrow."

"Don't worry about it." Her genuine concern only made my shame more humiliating. "I'll take care of it."

I hung my head out the window and let the wind slap my face into sobriety.

Several weeks later, I accepted a receptionist position at Rose-Magwood Productions, a thriving commercial production house with offices in London, Chicago, New York, Toronto, and California. They created commercials with Jonathan Winters, a successful comedian, Don Adams, the star of the *Get Smart* television series, the famous *Sports Illustrated* swimsuit model Cheryl Tiegs, and Jack Gilford of the popular Cracker Jack commercials. I wanted to learn every aspect of the industry—in front of and behind the cameras.

A young actress I met at work invited me to share her two-story home in the Hollywood Hills. I didn't want to intrude on Patty's hospitality any longer than necessary, so the timing was perfect.

In the meantime, Patty went to war with Rona Barrett's *Hollywood Magazine* for printing slanderous allegations about her relationship with Desi.

"I'll sue her for one penny," Patty said. "It's about principle and the truth." She paced back and forth. "It's not fair what they're saying." Desi's mom, Lucille Ball, stoked the tabloid fires in her disapproval of the relationship, and that added pressure contributed to their breakup.

The loss devastated Patty, but her trouble didn't stop there. "I lost Desi's baby . . . I wanted his baby . . . our baby." I could feel her heart breaking. "The doctors said it was in my fallopian tubes, and I could have died." Her emotions vacillated from tears to fury. I listened and empathized with her pain.

Several weeks later, I dropped by to check on her. She opened the door and demanded, "Who sent you?"

"Who sent me?" I said. "Nobody—I'm here to see how you're doing." Her bizarre attitude shocked me.

She waved me in with her glass of wine. I introduced myself to a group of people I didn't know while Patty's conversation jumped around in unconnected directions. I understood where these bits and pieces came from—fragments of her life experiences cast out in no cohesive order. Moreover, the strangers didn't seem to care about Patty as they drank her wine and ate her food. This disturbed me, and I left her apartment bewildered. How could I help my friend? What happened to her? I felt helpless.

Patty ran off to Las Vegas and married a man she barely knew named Michael Tell. The tabloids were full of speculations about her bizarre thirteen-day marriage. They ripped her apart. No one knew, including Patty, that she had a manic episode. Unfortunately, I lost contact with her after that. She disappeared into a sea of unknown people, and never answered phone calls, and disconnected from the world we knew.

Patty later discovered she suffered from manic depression, which caused her years of emotional torment. She received proper treatment and later coauthored a book about the disorder, *A Brilliant Madness: Living with Manic-Depressive Illness.*

Our lives led us in two different directions, but we both ended up advocating for mental health. I thought one day we might reconnect and share our journeys. We each found the answers that made sense for our lives. Sadly, her life ended before we had that chance.

Every day held new surprises at work—new projects, new actors, and unique opportunities for learning. Sid Caesar, the iconic comedian of the TV program *The Show of Shows*, contracted for a series of commercials and took offices in our production house. He brought H.F. Green, his manager, along with him. H.F., a Broadway character actor, always brightened my day. He resembled a New York gangster with his shiny bald head, thick black mustache, and pinstriped suits. But his quick wit kept all of us in stitches, and his kindness endeared him to everyone. He soon became a great friend. I grew to rely on his wisdom, and he became an important part of my life.

My work at Rose-Magwood Productions put me in the middle of one of the most competitive markets in show business. A national commercial can be extremely lucrative. It's what every actor hopes for, aside from a starring role in a movie or TV series. But when only one person is selected—out of hundreds—the competition becomes fierce. Desperate to succeed, it's hard for these talented, enthusiastic, young actors to realize they are often nothing more than expendable furniture.

The talent signed in at my desk for auditions. When we filmed a toy commercial, the lobby filled with stage mothers who coached their kids, "Make sure you smile at the nice man and do *everything* he says." They tucked in their kids' rumpled shirts and slicked back their hair. I saw first-hand that patience is not a virtue that children possess. "Stop that! Don't fidget," came the frequent rebukes during the long wait to be called.

When we filmed a beauty product, the models secretly assessed their competition. Pretending to fix her lipstick, one model used the mirror to look over her shoulder at the other beauties in the waiting room. The insecurities that lay hidden behind those slender bodies and bright smiles often slipped out.

Donna, a lovely young actress who had worked for our company in the past, auditioned for the national commercial we were casting. After her audition, she cornered Jim, the director, to see if she could persuade him to hire her for the job. "Maybe if you were a blond," he said, trying to let her down easy.

The next day we were finishing up the casting call, and she rushed in, almost unrecognizable. "Where's Jim?"

"In his office." I pointed to the door. Oh, boy, would he be surprised. Donna had her long brown hair dyed blond in hopes of getting the job! Unfortunately, another actress had already been hired.

I worked my way from receptionist to assistant casting director to production assistant. Working behind the scenes, learning what directors and clients looked for fascinated me, giving me a new perspective on the craft of filmmaking.

Acting challenged me on many levels and taught me a lot. I enjoyed the workshops, improvisational exercises, and the creative process. However intimidating, it helped me identify with different characters and break through my own self-consciousness. I signed with a talent agency and concentrated on commercials. I thought it would be fun. What did I know?

Chapter Five:
Brokenhearted Confusion

WHOSE LIFE SHOULD I SAVE?

He heals the brokenhearted
and binds up their wounds.

Psalm 147:3

Hollywood continued to reel from the gruesome Charles Manson murders. The murders included Sharon Tate, the eight-months pregnant wife of Roman Polanski, Jay Sebring, her hairdresser and former boyfriend, and four others. It stunned the world, and even after the murder trial convicted Manson and the "family," the news continued to unfold this bazaar tragedy. Years later, Quentin Tarantino wrote and directed his version of events in his film *Once Upon a Time in Hollywood*.

Jim, a young man from New Mexico who studied with Jay, came to California after the murders to purchase the Sebring hair salon. Despite the complications surrounding the sale, Jim determined to be Jay's successor and carry on his legacy.

Jim established himself as an accomplished hairstylist in his own right, but Jay's clientele included iconic names like Paul Newman, Peter Lawford, Frank Sinatra, and Steve McQueen. These were giant shoes for this small-town boy to fill.

A mutual friend introduced us, and Jim soon overcame my initial resistance with his charming persistence. His soft-spoken demeanor concealed a determined drive that finally persuaded me to leave my independence behind and move in with him.

As a child, Jim slept with the lights on and a knife under his pillow. He had a troubled childhood but managed to keep his insecurities well-hidden as he serviced Jay's elite client roster. Even when his issues unraveled, I didn't recognize their danger until too late.

Jim usually included me when he met his clients for house calls. "I'm on my way to the Beverly Hills Hotel. I'll pick you up in thirty minutes?"

On our drive to the hotel, Jim said, "Paul Newman's in town. He wanted to know if I could 'fit him in.'" We laughed at the thought of anyone saying "no" to Paul.

We arrived at his bungalow and found a note on the door, "Come to bungalow #1—PL."

Jim and I did as instructed and knocked on the back door of the bungalow. A sweet lilting laughter filled the night air as an enormous man with a deep voice answered.

"Yes," he said through the screen.

"Is Paul here?" Jim said.

"Paul, it's for you," the man boomed over his shoulder.

The screen door made it difficult to recognize the man. The door swung open, and out sprang Paul. He flung his arm around me and nodded to Jim.

"When are you going to come and go with the fox?" he teased as we headed down the tree-lined path to his bungalow. I smiled and looked for Jim. We entered the cozy bungalow, and Jim chose a place to set up his equipment while I made my way to the pale-yellow couch in front of the fireplace.

"Anyone for a glass of wine?" Paul said. We accepted. Paul ducked into the kitchen and returned with two glasses in hand. He placed Jim's near his table and stood in front of me while he swirled the wine in his right hand and then took a sip.

"Mmm . . . good," he said with his sensual blue eyes boring into mine. He bent down as I reached to take it and seductively whispered, "The next time I see you, it'll be in a bubble bath." This certainly wouldn't go over well with the #metoo movement of today, but back then this was *normal* for Hollywood.

My face flushed with warmth while those piercing blue eyes continued their scrutinizing gaze. He grinned mischievously and slid next to me. He seemed to revel in making me blush with his playful attention. Jim, oblivious, continued setting up while Paul continued his lighthearted teasing. It seemed the more I blushed, the bigger he grinned.

"Ok, Paul . . . ready," Jim said.

Paul touched my thigh as he moved to the chair for his haircut.

"That bungalow you came to was mine before Liz and Richard checked in," Paul said. "The hotel didn't know she'd be arriving." *Was he talking about Elizabeth Taylor and Richard Burton?*

"When she checked in, she requested her favorite bungalow, but I'd already moved in." He took a sip of wine. "She wrote me a sweet little note asking if she and Richard could exchange bungalows with me. Before I could even respond, she had all my belongings brought here." He chuckled.

"Her husband died in a plane crash right before we started filming *Cat on a Hot Tin Roof*. She didn't make us lose one day of shooting."

He appeared to shake off the dark memory with another sip of wine then grinned, "So whatever Liz wants, she can have."

The tone of his voice reflected their strong bond of friendship.

Paul had formed a production company with John Foreman, the producer of *Butch Cassidy and the Sundance Kid*. Their first project under the Newman-Foreman banner was *Pocket Money* with Lee Marvin.

Filming started on location in Arizona, and Paul flew us down for the weekend. Paul's wife, Joanne Woodward, also arrived that weekend. During a break in the shooting, Paul introduced us to her.

"Did Jim cut your hair?" Joanne said. She pushed back the headband that kept her long blond hair from falling in her face.,

"Yes," I said.

"Jim, could you style my hair like that?" She picked up a section of her hair. "I need to do something with this."

"Sure, I'd love to." Off they went for a wash and cut while I went for the electric rollers.

After Jim cut her hair, I showed Joanne how to use the rollers to complete the style. We giggled like two kids at a sleepover.

She swung her new curls. "I love it."

Later that day, Paul found us in the hotel coffee shop, "I have to fly back to LA, so why don't you use my suite?" He handed Jim the key. "Have fun. I'll see you later." He rushed off before we could say, "Thank you."

Jim had one last appointment with Lee Marvin before we returned to Los Angeles. Lee, a larger-than-life, charismatic storyteller, kept everyone engrossed with his nonstop wit and outrageous stories. With his volcanic personality, he definitely became a force you didn't want to reckon with. Yet, when he took a moment to breathe, his sweetness slipped out just a smidge before he returned to center stage.

After Jim finished cutting Lee's hair, we headed to Paul's suite. Jim opened the door to Paul's inner sanctum and peeked inside. The smiling faces of his wife and children greeted us, enshrined on his dresser in their silver frames. They created an intimacy that ushered us into a corner of Paul's heart. We didn't dare touch his large portable sauna but instead drank a toast to him from his large jug of organic apple juice.

When we returned to Los Angeles, Jim and his two business partners ran into trouble. Jim wanted to pursue a new line of products, but he had difficulty raising the finances. The pressure mounted, and, unbeknownst to me, he grew dependent on drugs.

This was when things changed—the fights, the jealous rages, and the abuse. Jim kept me up all night when he knew I had a modeling job the next day. That forced me to take pills to make it through the shoot. As the insanity increased, it became harder for drugs not to infiltrate my life. If Jim ran out of words, he became aggressive and shook me, threw me on the couch or up against the wall. The more pressure—the more drugs—the more intense the abuse.

A disagreement began over breakfast in a local restaurant. A sharp pain jolted my shin and brought tears to my eyes.

"What?" I didn't understand.

"Let's go," he grabbed my arm and pulled me from the booth. We reached the parking lot, and he shoved me into his black Porsche. Still annoyed, he zoomed out of the parking lot and raced up Laurel Canyon.

"Slow down Jim, you're going to kill us!" I braced my feet against the floor. He skidded around a turn, and I slammed against the door.

"Jim, you're being crazy. Stop!" The car spun out of control, and we crashed into an embankment. He threw the gear into reverse and backed the car off the hill and sped home. Shaken with fear, my clammy hands gripped the edges of my seat.

I don't know why I didn't end it right then, but Jim's pain held me captive. I cared more for him than I did for myself. I didn't know how to set boundaries or consequences for certain behaviors. I made excuses for him, which only enabled his destructive behaviors.

I was determined to get him help, but I had no idea what help even looked like. Addiction and recovery were not words I understood. The only drugs I knew were the recreational ones floating around in the 60s. The thought of Jim being addicted never entered my mind. That's how naïve I was.

The fighting wore me down, and my only relief came when he left for work. Only then did I have a few hours of peace and quiet—until he returned. After an angry disagreement, I sat in the stairwell outside the apartment and thought, *I can stay here and try to save* his *life, or I can leave and save* my own *life.* This should have been an obvious choice—right? Wrong. Fear had paralyzed my damaged emotions.

I knew I couldn't continue to live with him unless he got help. When I threatened to leave him, he finally agreed to make an appointment to see a psychiatrist. A flicker of hope raised its head, and I thanked the doctor for seeing us.

"I'll try to get Jim to come back." The doctor looked at me with concern.

"What about you? Why don't you come back?"

What did he mean? I didn't have a problem. Jim did. And now he'd get help. Why would I need therapy?

We walked out of the office and never returned. The doctor's question troubled me. Later I understood his reference to my classic codependent behavior. I was as sick as Jim for putting up with his abusive behavior.

The conflicts continued to escalate. After Jim left for work, I sat on the couch with the T.V. clicker, ready to distract myself with mindless entertainment, when I heard a voice inside my head say, "Call H.F."

I had a choice: either numb myself or find my life.

"Call H.F."

There's that voice again. *H.F. Green, my friend from the production company?*

"Yes—call him."

Dear God, let him be home. The relief of hearing his voice brought me to tears.

"Get your things together. I'm on my way," he responded immediately. "Don't worry about anything."

H.F.'s strength gave me the courage to leave. What would Jim do when he discovered I left? Would he track me down as he had before? Like a child in the protective custody of her father, I breathed a sigh of relief and whispered a silent prayer of gratitude.

Chapter Six:
Self Esteem for Sale

WHAT HAPPENED TO DIGNITY?

Because you received a double dose of shame and dishonor,
you will inherit a double portion of endless joy
and everlasting bliss!

Isaiah 61:7 TPT

Safely hidden in my trusted friend's guest room, I still couldn't stop the fearful thoughts. Visions of Jim running me over with his car plagued me every time I left the house—which wasn't often. My reactions mirrored a frightened animal searching for any perceived threat. No matter where I went, I needed an exit strategy for an easy escape.

The fear of Jim finding me kept me from speaking to anyone who knew him. In the past, he had manipulated my girlfriends to find out where I was but not this time. He didn't know H.F., and I knew I'd be protected.

"It'll be okay, Pam," H.F. assured me. "You'll get through this."

I wanted to believe him, but my fear didn't see how.

He listened for hours as my mind ruminated on the same chaotic scenarios, searching for answers.

"What's wrong with me?" I said.

H.F. touched my hand and with great compassion said, "I think you've lost your self-esteem."

His words hit me in the gut like a baseball bat. *What? How do you lose your self-esteem? Is there a two-for-one sale somewhere . . . anywhere?* His comment left me naked with nothing to cover my shame—only more questions.

I finally felt strong enough to risk having lunch with a friend. After I shared my story with her, she said, "Pam, do you think maybe God is talking to you through H.F.?"

The question stunned me. What an epiphany! Adrenaline rushed through me. "Do you mean God speaks through people like he did through his disciples in the days of the Bible?"

My head exploded, and a spiritual portal opened and thrust me into an entirely new world. A supernatural clarity seemed to sharpen even my natural vision. I never experienced anything like this. God supernaturally, dramatically touched me. My friend twisted her napkin and avoided my eyes. She became transparent as I connected to the tenderness of her heart.

My eyes welled with tears. I never thought to listen for God's voice through other people. God only spoke through preachers on Sunday. This day, God stepped off the pulpit and into my life. He became a real presence to discover in everyday life.

I had no one to explain this powerful spiritual experience. I never heard the term "born-again" and had no idea what it meant to surrender my life to Jesus. I just knew that God was real and he helped me. A flood of new life engulfed me with a sense of exhilarating joy. For a little while, the darkness lifted, and hope opened a window.

In his long black robes, Reverend Lloyd Ogilvie of the Hollywood Presbyterian Church, preached with such a deep theatrical voice and dramatic flair that I thought he might be an out-of-work actor. His thick black hair and chiseled face made him handsome enough. I resonated with the depth of his message after my spiritual encounter. His powerful sermons nourished my fledgling faith, but the long drive from the San Fernando Valley made it difficult to attend church regularly. He later left Hollywood and became the Senate Chaplain in Washington.

My life changed, and I wanted to share my new revelations with my girlfriends. I thought they'd be excited for me. But maybe the Polo Lounge at the Beverly Hills Hotel wasn't the best place to talk about God.

After I shared my experience, my friends responded, "That's nice, Pam."

That's nice, Pam? That's all they had to say?

I ordered another Brandied Alexander and lit my cigarette.

"Don't you believe in God?" I said.

"Sure, but you have to admit that's pretty incredible." Their less than enthusiastic response disappointed me.

"Of course, it is...I know it is, but it's true." *How could I make them understand?* "This isn't about religion. It's personal." I wanted to defend myself. "I know God did something and showed up like I've never experienced him before." My Lutheran upbringing gave me fundamental beliefs but did not explain a personal encounter with God. I never felt God's presence when I went to church. It seemed more like a social obligation than anything else.

"All I know is what happened." I put my cigarette out, and they changed the subject.

"Why don't they get it?" I asked H.F. when I arrived home. "They didn't seem interested, or maybe they didn't believe me." I wanted them to discover the same joy I experienced.

"Don't worry about it." H.F. reassured me. "God's been defending himself for thousands of years. I think he can handle it." H.F. was Jewish with a spiritual sensitivity but wasn't familiar with New Testament Christianity.

Without a Christian community to nurture my spiritual growth my newfound faith began to fade into the background.

I continually wrestled with accusing thoughts as I tried to make sense of my past relationship. How could I be so stupid? Could I ever trust anyone again? Hope tried to fight through a small crack in the growing darkness, but it didn't have enough strength to silence these accusations.

Lying on my bed, I fell into a twilight sleep—that faint, diffused sleep where your body is at rest but your mind is alert. I pictured myself as a three-year-old child sleeping at the feet of Jesus under a large tree on a grassy knoll. I didn't feel worthy enough to look into his eyes, much less crawl onto his lap like children often do.

I rested my head on his nail-scarred feet, using them as my pillow, and took hold of the hem of his garment. I held it close to my cheek as though it were my childhood blanket. Being this close to Jesus dispelled my fears. Amid this idyllic scene, a dividing line mysteriously appeared. The ground separated, forming a deep crevasse. On the other side, a figure covered in a flowing black-hooded cape came galloping toward us on a huge black stallion. The powerful stallion stomped the ground as it came to the edge of the chasm. I froze, paralyzed with fear. Satan's come to get me!

In a panic, I pleaded with Jesus, "Make him go away!"

Jesus whispered, "No, you make him go away."

"What? I can't make this powerful demon go away."

I mustered all the courage I could find in my trembling little body and put one hesitant foot in front of the other, creeping to the edge of the dividing line. I pushed out a weak, "Go away," but he didn't move.

Smoke billowed from the stallion's nostrils as he reared and pounded the ground. The blood-red eyes of the rider pierced me like daggers. I ran back to Jesus and frantically leaped up and down in panic.

"He didn't go away! Make him go away, Jesus!" I pulled on his robe in stark terror.

With great patience but firm resolve, Jesus turned me around, gently nudged me towards my adversary, and said, "You make him go away."

Again, I bravely gathered my courage and tottered back. I shouted, "Satan, get thee behind me, in Jesus' name!" I spun around and ran back to Jesus, sliding between his feet like a baseball player sliding into home base.

I woke to the safety of my bed, and the images disappeared. What just happened? Was that real? I wondered what it meant.

Why didn't Jesus fight for me? Why did he send me, a child, to face that formidable evil force? Maybe he wanted to show me that his name—the name of Jesus—has more power than anyone can imagine, so powerful that even a child has authority in his name.

As I stepped out in faith, Jesus stood behind me. He gave me the courage to combat my fear, face the evil confronting me, and experience relief in his name. "All your children will be taught by the LORD, and great will be their peace" (Isaiah 54:13).

Even with this powerful imagery, I didn't understand the significance of its implications. God would continue to build on this revelation until it became the muscular reality needed to fend off the negative influences of darkness with all its false accusations, lies, fearful thoughts, and confusion. It had to start with me first.

We demolish arguments and every pretension that sets itself up against the knowledge of God, and we take captive every thought to make it obedient to Christ. (2 Corinthians 10:5)

Chapter Seven

The Kingdoms of the World

TOO MUCH FOOL'S GOLD

*Again, the devil took Him up on an exceedingly high mountain,
and showed Him all the kingdoms of the world and their glory.
And he said to Him, "All these things I will give You if You
will fall down and worship me."*

*Then Jesus said to him, "Away with you, Satan! For it is
written, 'You shall worship the LORD your God, and Him only
you shall serve.'"*

Matthew 4:8-10 NKJV

Over time, I grew stronger and finally emerged from my
protective cocoon. I didn't know how to process my
encounters with God, and I didn't have a mature Christian to
help me understand the world of the spirit. H.F. believed in the Jewish
God of the Old Testament but wasn't familiar with Jesus.

God touched my damaged heart when I didn't even know how to
pray. I wasn't looking for him, but he showed up to help me move past
the fear that had crippled me for months. It felt good to be alive again.

My friends didn't want to hear about God, so he slipped out of the
conversations. Life went back to "normal," and I hid my encounters with
God in my heart.

My friends invited me to dinner and chose Joe Allen's, a Hollywood
hot spot where industry folks fraternized over burgers and beer. We sat
at the bar waiting for our table when a well-dressed, distinguished man
strolled in and greeted us.

"Ed, this is Pam," my friend said. The intensity in his eyes ignited a
spark I wasn't prepared for. "Ed's a writer for the *Mary Tyler Moore Show*."

"I love that show," I smiled.

"Me too." His contagious laughter disarmed me. I didn't expect this sophisticated man to have such a playful charm. We chatted for a few minutes before he asked for my number. A few days later, he called to ask me to dinner. It didn't take long before he captivated my heart. We fell in love and quickly became a couple. His nuanced view of life spotted the humorous aspects of human behavior, and his intelligent wit made him a prolific comedy writer.

Grant Tinker, Mary Tyler Moore's husband, hired Jim Brooks and Allen Burns to create a show for her under MTM Productions. They developed the *Mary Tyler Moore Show* and added Ed and his partner to the writing and producing staff. Ed later moved to Paramount Pictures and started the John Charles Walters Company along with Jim Brooks, where they created *Taxi* and other acclaimed TV sitcoms. Their energy and creativity flooded the airwaves, and everything they developed made television history.

Ed had written a cameo spot for Betty Ford to appear on the *Mary Tyler Moore Show*. The first lady agreed, and the crew planned to fly to Washington, DC, to film the episode. Mary and Mrs. Ford were both stepping into new roles. Mrs. Ford, the actress, and Mary, the animal rights activist. Mary planned on taking advantage of this time to testify before the Senate subcommittee, encouraging them to ban the cruel use of leghold traps on animals.

I just finished taking Angus, Ed's German Shepard, for a walk and was about to feed our animals when the phone rang. I was delighted to hear Ed's voice. He had to work late but called to ask, "How would you like to come to Washington with us?"

"Really?" I said. "I'd love to." His thoughtful kindness touched me.

My head started swimming with what to pack for such an auspicious occasion. I didn't have time to shop for something special since we were leaving in a couple of days. What do you wear to the White House to meet the first lady, anyway?

Mary, her husband Grant, Ed, and I landed in Washington tense with nervous expectation. The next day we arrived at the White House, greeted by several White House staff. The halls were alive with history.

The ghosts of the great leaders who once inhabited this citadel of power still resided here. The White House photographer persistently snapped photos along the way.

"I want a picture of me mowing the lawn in the backyard," quipped Ed with a chuckle.

"Step this way, please," our guide said as the secret service ushered us into a private elevator.

"Where are they taking us?" I whispered to Ed.

A secret service man turned to answer, "Upstairs to the private living quarters to meet the first lady." The reality of the moment unnerved me as we stepped across the foyer into the presidential living room.

The statuesque first lady, Mrs. Ford, stood in front of the living room's enormous arched window while we stood frozen at the entrance to the room. The several seconds of awkward silence prompted me to ask, "Is Susan still enjoying her photography?" I had read an article in *Newsweek* that her daughter had taken up photography.

"Oh, yes, she came back from the Grand Canyon, where she took the most amazing photos." Mrs. Ford smiled and stepped toward us.

"How wonderful," I continued. "Did you do the decorating?"

"No, we left it the way it was except for the dining room." We moved further into the living room. "The wallpaper was too dark, so we changed it. Would you like to see it?"

We followed her into the dining room like a row of dedicated penguins. By this time, the others gave up their search for something significant to say and entered into the conversation. I retreated to my observer status with great relief.

I sensed an undertone of sadness in Mrs. Ford. What must it be like for her and her family? She seemed to carry a weight beyond that of her position. Later we learned she battled with alcoholism and eventually founded the Betty Ford Treatment Center.

After lunch, we proceeded to a nearby hotel to film Mrs. Ford's cameo. The secret service surrounded us at every step. Ed, the consummate professional, patiently gave Mrs. Ford directions as he positioned her on the couch. He handed her the phone she needed to speak her lines into. Mrs. Ford struggled with her lines, and Mary came to the rescue. She knelt in front of her to offer encouragement.

The significance of the moment compelled me to approach them. I knelt beside Mary and said, "It's an honor for me to watch the first lady of our country exchange places with the first lady of comedy." They both smiled, and Mary patted my knee in appreciation.

After they finished filming, we headed to the airport. Everyone sat in silence as the limousine sped away. When we arrived at the airport, Mary said, "Do you want to stop by the studio tomorrow to talk about the trip?"

"Thank you, Mary, but I have some friends I can share this with." I appreciated her kindness but didn't want to take away from her moment. This was her story to share with her cast and crew.

Grant hugged me goodbye and said, "You did good, Pam."

"Thank you, Grant." I appreciated his acknowledgment.

What an indelible moment in history—from the cornfields of the Midwest to the historical halls of the White House. Where on earth did I find the courage to speak up and start a relevant conversation with the first lady? I surprised myself with these spontaneous moments that came out of nowhere. I never imagined I'd have such an honor.

First lady Betty Ford - Mary Tyler Moore - Me - Grant Tinker

Acting provided a creative outlet, but I didn't take it seriously. I enjoyed the creative challenge but I didn't have the burning ambition needed to make it a successful career choice. Without that driving desire to be famous it's hard to make it in this town. So, I always kept a side job to supplement my income. I picked up work with Brian, a young English man who sold antique English pub mirrors at his shop on Sunset Boulevard. The flexible hours gave me the freedom to go on auditions. "I've sold some of my artwork to a friend in London," Brian said. "It will pay for your trip to London and the new merchandise we need for the store."

"You want me to go?" He shocked me. "I've never been to London." I'd never even been to Europe.

"Yes, you can stay with my mum in South Kensington, and I'll give you my business contacts. You know what the store needs. I have business to finish here."

It came at an opportune time since Ed and I had some ridiculous fight and had separated again. I needed a distraction to relieve the pain. Our relationship was never easy. Exciting—yes, but easy—not always. Since I didn't know how to resolve conflicts or communicate feelings in a healthy way I chose to run if I thought I might be hurt, which caused more hurt in the long term.

When I told H.F. about my trip to London, he said, "My friend Vincent Gardenia is starring in the Broadway play *God's Favorite*. Why don't I make arrangements for you to meet Vince and see the play during your stopover in New York?"

"That sounds like fun. I've never seen a Broadway play."

The excitement of Times Square didn't match the excitement I felt as I entered the theater. The Neil Simon play was a modern interpretation of the Biblical account of Job. I enjoyed the play and Vince's performance. He invited me to an after-show party with the cast and other Broadway actors that lasted into the wee hours of the morning.

Exhausted and still hung-over, I arrived at JFK in need of coffee. There were no open restaurants in the deserted airport at this early hour. I placed the artwork behind an empty counter and went in search of the much-needed caffeine. I hiked some distance from the gate before I found a small café with freshly brewed coffee. When I heard my flight announced, I bolted for the gate. Once on board, I promptly fell asleep. Somewhere over the Atlantic, I shot straight up. The artwork hadn't left New York! In a panic, I grabbed the stewardess.

"Let me talk to the captain," she said, "He can call back to the airport and see if they can locate it."

"Thank you—without it my trip is useless." She took my name and number.

"The airlines will call and let you know if they find it. That's all we can do for now." I sank back in my seat to fight off a barrage of condemning thoughts.

Brian's mother, a small, plump English woman, lived in a lovely three-story flat in South Kensington with a small columned white porch that replicated all the other quaint porches lining the street. I didn't understand why the living room was on the first floor and the kitchen on the second floor. It took a while to adjust to this new environment.

The next day the airline called with good news—they found the artwork. I collapsed into the overstuffed chair and let out a sigh of relief. They shipped the artwork in time to complete the scheduled sale. I finally had the money to buy the merchandise to ship back to California.

Brian's friends were helpful and taught me how to use public transportation, which allowed me to better navigate the city. I felt like a native Londoner hopping on a double decker bus or grabbing the underground to go to the flea markets or meet a friend for tea. Even with new people and experiences, I desperately missed Ed, who didn't know I had left the country.

Elaine Stritch was starring in *The Gingerbread Lady,* a Neil Simon play. Ed had introduced us when she guest-starred on Mary's TV show, and I decided to see her play. Afterwards I called Ed to tell him Elaine sent her warmest regards. Ed sounded glad to hear from me.

"I have meetings in New York, but I could fly to Paris if you can meet me."

"I'd love to. Where should I meet you?"

"I'll be there next week. Meet me at the George V hotel." I hung up the phone, light-headed from the adrenaline rush. Ed's meeting me in Paris! I couldn't wait to see him. After arriving in Paris, we spent the next few days restoring our relationship.

Ed, a connoisseur of fine dining, chose La Tour d'Argent, a historic restaurant famous for its duck. The restaurant overlooked the Seine, and its elegant décor and soft lighting made for a romantic ambiance. Sharing this with Ed brought a warm glow of contentment. He reached for my hand and gazed into my eyes.

"Do you know what this means, Pam?"

I thought it meant he loved me, so I nodded yes.

Caught up in the beauty of the moment, I didn't think to say, "No, Ed, what does this mean?" It would have been the perfect time for a deeper conversation about the future of our relationship. The damaged remnants of my past still stood guard over my heart, making it difficult to press into those fragile places of intimacy. All I knew is he loved me and flew to Paris to be with me.

After Ed left for Los Angeles, the loneliness of our empty hotel room left me paralyzed. Barely able to function, I forced myself back to London to finish shipping the container. It would take another couple of weeks before I could fly home. I couldn't wait.

After returning from London, the next few months were a passionate reunion with Ed. Living in that tenuous place of loving vulnerability created an internal tension that left me defenseless. When old patterns began to reemerge, fear caused my protective walls to resurrect. My emotional alarm bells went off, and they were stronger than my ability to understand or control them. The moments we connected were glorious, but when we couldn't, it became excruciating.

My emotions built up, and I'd do crazy things. Once, I stormed out of the house in tears, defiantly carrying Jennifer, our little kitten, bouncing around in her litter box. Then there was the time I plunged a knife into the center of the butcher block after slamming down the phone to make my point. Because I didn't know how to deal with the conflict directly, I acted it out.

"I thought you meant that knife for me," Ed said, as we laughed about it later. I never considered myself a drama queen, but apparently, I had my moments. Love is a complex dance of emotions. If past hurts are left unattended, they continue to bleed into the present.

Ed had to fly to Europe for an awards dinner and didn't invite me to join him. This scorned woman had a brilliant idea to send a few mementos of her own. Embarrassed but determined, I did something I never imagined myself doing. I went to a sex shop and bought two funny cards and a deck of playing cards with risqué photos on the front. My favorite item was a book of matches that looked like any ordinary book of matches, but when opened, what popped up was a part of the male anatomy.

Ed's suitcase lay half-filled on the bedroom couch. I carefully placed my purchases in various suit pockets so when he dressed, he'd discover my surprises. The book of pop-up matches deserved a special place in the pocket of his elegant tuxedo jacket. I knew he'd offer to light some woman's cigarette at the event. Oh, to see their faces when he did!

When Ed returned home, he never said a word. And I never asked. But his suit pockets were empty.

Vincent Gardenia, H.F.'s friend, signed on for a film in Rome and wanted H.F. to go with him. Ed and I were struggling, and this time our relationship seemed strained beyond repair.

"What am I going to do?" I said when H.F. told me. "You're the only one I can talk to." H.F. kept me anchored with his clear-headed wisdom.

"Let me talk to Vince. I'm sure there's something for you in the movie."

Janis, my long-time friend, lived across the hall in my apartment building. She worked as an executive at Capitol Records, and we attended many industry parties together. As one of my best friends, she understood my struggles with Ed.

"Janis, I'm going to Rome," I said. "I have to get away."

"What? When?"

"In a few weeks."

"I have vacation time coming up. Why don't I come with you?"

"Great! I'd love it."

The thought of being surrounded by friends made me less anxious, and traveling with Janis would be fun. I needed to divert my thoughts away from my failing relationship with Ed.

I unexpectedly bumped into Marty Elfand, the head of motion picture production at Warner Brothers. He produced *Dog Day Afternoon* starring Al Pacino, which received multiple Academy-Award nominations, including Best Picture. Unfortunately, he lost the Oscar for Best Picture to Michael Douglas and Saul Zaentz who produced *One Flew Over the Cuckoo's Nest.*

We chatted, and he asked, "What are you up to?"

"I'm leaving for Rome in a few days."

"I'm leaving for London," he said. "Why don't you come with me? I have another meeting in Paris, and you could fly to Rome from there."

His invitation surprised me, and I resisted this abrupt change of plans.

"Thank you, but my friend Janis is coming with me. It's too late to change our plans."

"Don't worry. I'll make the arrangements for both of you."

After discussing this new turn of events with H.F. and Janis, no one seemed to have any objections. Vincent assured H.F. I wouldn't be needed in Rome for a couple of weeks, so we had time to make the trip to London.

Janis and I spent two delightful days in London exploring the city while Marty attended meetings. In the evenings, Marty took us to fabulous restaurants, and we explored London's exciting nightlife.

When we arrived in Paris, Marty had arranged for rooms at the George V Hotel and placed a limousine at our disposal. We picked through treasures at the flea market, drove through the Arc de Triomphe, waved at the Louvre, and shopped. We packed a week's worth of sightseeing into one day.

"Marty, thank you for everything," I said as we waited for the car to take us to the airport. "It's been fantastic." I gave him a hug and kissed him goodbye.

"Thanks for letting me tag along," Janis said, "It's been amazing." She gave him a hug.

"Listen, I have to be back in Europe for the Cannes Film Festival—if you're still here, why don't you come with me?" I appreciated Marty's offer. The festival is a major industry event.

"I don't know what our filming schedule is, so I'll have to let you know," I said.

"Great! I'll call you." He smiled. We hugged, and he waved goodbye as the car pulled away.

After the beauty of Paris, Rome appeared disturbingly shabby, full of graffiti and ancient ruins. Nonetheless, it didn't take long before the historical beauty of Rome made it my favorite European city.

I fell in love with the Coliseum, the Sistine chapel, the enormity of the Vatican with all the great artists' paintings, and the incredible fountains throughout the city. The people had a robust quality of life.

Janis and I spent our days on the set or exploring the shops. After a late afternoon nap, we dressed for dinner at ten p.m., then off to the nightclubs to dance until the early morning: our European lifestyle turned into a magical escapade.

I felt a pang of loneliness when Janis returned home, but Vince and H.F. kept life exciting. We each had a private apartment at the Residence Aldrovandi. In the mornings after Vince left for the studio, H.F. and I strolled through the beautiful Villa Borghese gardens, down the Spanish steps, to the Piazza del Popolo for cappuccino and breakfast. Sitting in the outdoor café and drinking in the culture with my friend made life significantly richer. I contemplated living in Rome after the film finished but didn't have the courage to stay on my own. Things were still unresolved in Los Angeles.

"There's a break in the shooting schedule," Vince said, "and the studio gave me a car. Let's drive to Naples."

"Vinny was born in Naples before his family moved to Brooklyn," H.F. said.

"How fun." I couldn't wait to see more of the Italian countryside.

Once we arrived, we wandered the streets and drank in the crisp sea air as we searched for a place to dine. "This looks good," Vince said.

He decided on a dark atmospheric cabaret with a piano bar and rustic Italian stone decor. "Neapolitan pizza is the best in the world." He ordered everything on the menu. We devoured pizza, pasta, fish, and an assortment of other savory delights washed down with bottles of wine.

Our hunger satisfied, we relaxed, a little light-headed from the wine. The Broadway actors took over the piano bar and sang old show tunes to everyone's delight. H.F. sat cross-legged on top of the piano, preening and pretending to understand Vincent's Italian while they improvised antics. The patrons sang along, laughing and drinking like a big Italian family. As the morning sun rose over the glistening water, we meandered along the Bay of Naples, captivated by the beauty of the dawn.

We drove the short distance to the top of Mount Vesuvius overlooking the city of Pompeii, once destroyed by the volcano's eruption. This spectacular view brought tears to my eyes—a perfect end to one of life's memorable moments. Arrivederci, Napoli! We returned to Rome for the last week of shooting before returning to America.

The film wrapped, and Vince and H.F. returned to Los Angeles. Marty convinced me to stay until he arrived, and then we'd fly to France for the film festival. He landed the day after Vince and H.F. left. It took two days of shopping in Rome before finding the perfect designer gown for the festival's opening.

We checked into the Carlton Hotel in Nice, bustling with photographers, publicists, and all kinds of film types enthusiastic to network and shop their products. Cannes' quaint, romantic charm disappeared as this influx of people from all over the world carpeted the streets.

MGM'S Film, *That's Entertainment, Part II*, opened the festival. Kirk Kerkorian, who bought MGM pictures in the 1960s, flew over with many of the film stars. He hosted a lunch at the Hôtel du Cap Eden Roc on the French Riviera in Antibes. Seated at a table filled with iconic film legends like Fred Astaire, Gene Kelly, and the major money giants behind the studios gave me a candid view of what worldly power and pride look like. Their credentials certainly earned them those rights but only exaggerated the lack of my own. I sat unusually silent, smiling, listening, and observing this unique glimpse into the ruling class of the cinema.

Marty flew back to Los Angeles with the MGM crew on their private jet, and I flew to Wisconsin to visit my family before returning to Los Angeles. I stared out the plane window, reflecting on my recent experiences. *If I die tomorrow, I can say I lived a full and exciting life—I have done more, seen more, and experienced more than I ever could have imagined.*

After returning from Rome, Ed and I tried to make our relationship work, but too many unresolved issues made it impossible. I moved back to my apartment, but we remained friends. Marty and I continued to see each other, but it wasn't like me to become involved in another relationship until I sorted through the emotional wreckage of the last one. I couldn't fully embrace any new relationship while my heart continued to hemorrhage. I lost myself somewhere along the way and no longer recognized myself.

It seemed like Marty knew everyone in the entertainment business. He ran into celebrities wherever we went. His extroverted personality enjoyed socializing with people, and his genuine caring caused people to gravitate toward him.

We attended an intimate dinner party at Tina Sinatra's lovely home in Beverly Hills. Several small tables lit with candles surrounded the outdoor pool. After being ushered to my seat, I looked up . . . oh, my gosh. . . across from me sat Cary Grant, one of my favorite iconic actors.

"Hello," he said. "Lovely evening, isn't it?"

I smiled and managed to say, "Lovely." His devastating good looks and charming demeanor left me speechless.

Cary experimented with LSD and talked about how much he had enjoyed his experience. He said, "Timothy Leary believed LSD could be useful in psychiatry, and they used it at Harvard's Research Center." He mesmerized everyone with his fascinating stories. A few weeks later, Marty called, "How would you like to go to the Academy Awards?"

How could I refuse? I already had the designer dress from the Cannes Film Festival hanging in my closet. Marty arrived in the limousine, and we headed to the show.

"I'm not crazy about the rubber chicken at these events," Marty said. "Let's stop at Tommy's for a burger." He instructed the limo driver to head over to the hamburger stand. When we pulled up, Marty gave the driver our order. There we sat in the back seat of the limo in our elegant evening attire, munching down the best sloppy burgers in town.

After we finished, we headed over to the show and pulled up to the red carpet with its throng of people, press, and flashing light bulbs. The place swarmed with a sea of glamorous celebrities, dazzling smiles, and sparkling jewels. The pride and pretense were palpable. I drifted through the crowd like an invisible stranger observing this cast of masked players.

Rocky won the Oscar for Best Picture. Faye Dunaway won the Best Actress award and Peter Finch Best Actor, both from the film *Network*. I bumped into Ms. Dunaway and her Oscar in the women's lounge after the show.

"Well, hello, handsome," I said and rubbed the head of her bald-headed buddy. "Congratulations on your win tonight." Faye smiled, and we both giggled.

After the show, Marty and I headed to the Governor's Ball—the most star-studded evening in Hollywood. The burgers staved off our hunger during the lengthy show and made the less-than-appetizing dinner palatable. This was long before Wolfgang Puck became the chef for this dazzling affair.

While everything appeared glamorous from the outside, the dark void inside continued to consume me. If I had been more ambitious, maybe I could have used these opportunities to my advantage. Perhaps if I had a clear purpose, I wouldn't have lost myself in this world of power and intrigue.

Why didn't these exciting experiences fulfill me? They were only windows into lifestyles beyond my own. I struggled to make sense of it all. The more I interacted with the rich and famous, the more insignificant I felt—the more self-conscious I became of my inadequacies.

I found myself heading into a relationship with another powerful man who could render me more powerless than I already felt—a pattern seemed to be emerging that I had to break.

What am I doing? Would I keep going from one relationship to another under the false pretense of looking for love? Who *was* I? I heard the clock ticking.

Is there an elusive truth that holds the keys to love and fulfillment? Where are the answers that make sense of life? The many schools of thought and spirituality I tried only brought a temporary relief before they faded into the next new trend. Then there are the more self-destructive methods to numb the hopelessness born of continual disappointment.

I pursued the ways of the world and all its grandeur—that privileged world behind the golden doors—and I paid the price. I thought my dreams were coming true, but instead, they ravaged my soul. The smoke of puffed-up pride catered to my ego, all the while sucking the innocence right out of me. There must be more to life than the materialistic vanity of wealth, power, and fame.

*This photo is an acting headshot by Harry Langdon but
it reflects the growing unhappiness I felt at the time.*

I was fortunate in the early '70's to have photos taken by Harry Langdon, before he became a world-class celebrity photographer known for his backlit photos.

Once upon a time in a land far, far, away....

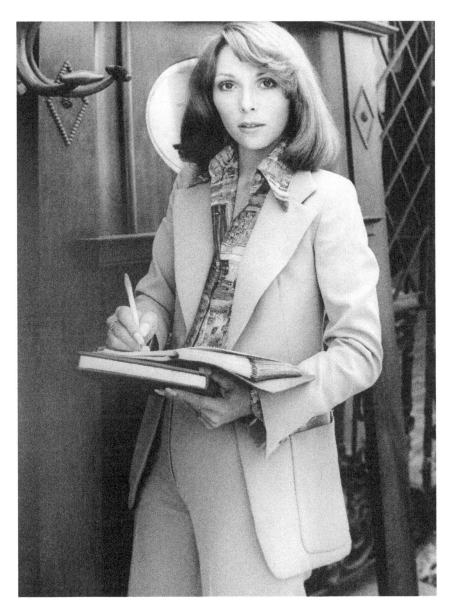

I wish I knew then what I know now…growing up is a learning experience.

The many faces of modeling—gotta love those shoes!

THE PATH
TO
TRANSFORMATION

Chapter Eight:
Let's Make a Deal

IS GOD WHO HE SAYS HE IS?

Purify your hearts, for your loyalty is divided between God and the world.

James 4:8 NLT

Don't copy the behavior and customs of this world, but let God transform you into a new person by changing the way you think. Then you will learn to know God's will for you, which is good and pleasing and perfect.

Romans 12:2 NLT

I returned to my neglected life to reassemble the pieces. It's tough going from the opulence of caviar and limousines back to McDonald's and Volkswagens. I stopped seeing Marty and wrapped myself in a protective blanket of isolation to examine what had happened to my life.

I tried to fight the growing hopelessness, but the weariness of my soul couldn't find the strength until one day when I reconnected with a former modeling friend.

"Hi, Pam, it's Cathy," the soft voice said on the other end of the phone.

"Cathy! It's so good to hear from you." Cathy and I met when I worked at the commercial production house.

"Can we get together?" I hadn't seen Cathy since being her maid of honor. She married Tony Eldridge, who later went on to produce *The Equalizer* with Denzel Washington.

"Absolutely." I looked forward to seeing my friend.

Tony greeted me with a hug when I arrived at their rustic cabin in Laurel Canyon; Cathy sat propped up by oversized flowered pillows in the bed that confined her. Her delicate features hadn't changed much, and her long brown hair still retained its shine despite her debilitating autoimmune disease. She spoke more about the church she attended called the Vineyard than she did about her physical condition. Her life had dramatically changed.

"We meet on the beach in Santa Monica," she said. "I can't go right now because of my condition, but you should go. You'd love it."

Who ever heard of a church that met on the beach? Or called itself the *Vineyard?* I kept my concerns to myself since she seemed so happy.

"Please go, Pam," she pleaded. "I want to know what you think,"

"Sure, Cathy, I'll try." I wanted to placate her. I didn't have the time or inclination to sit on the beach and listen to some cult leader talk about who knows what. Any church that met on a beach sounded cultish in my mind.

But Cathy genuinely seemed changed. Despite her condition, she had a new sense of hope reflected in her smile. She talked with such enthusiasm, it made me wonder what changed her. My Sunday school days taught me traditional Bible stories, and I considered myself a Christian, but the church she described didn't compute with my experience. I wanted to protect my friend from getting involved with some cult.

"Remember, Tony? The photographer?" she said.

"Of course, Tony Roller. He took some of the most beautiful pictures of us. I love his work."

"His wife caught him in an affair and wanted a divorce. When they began going to the church, they started working through their issues, and God restored their marriage."

"Really?" This piqued my interest.

"Why don't you meet them there?"

"Ok, I'll think about it."

Over a month had slipped by before I could attend. By that time, the church had moved from the beach to a 4:00 p.m. service at a Methodist church building located in the San Fernando Valley. What happened to Sunday morning services? This *church* seemed more like some kind of gypsy caravan.

I met Tony and his wife in the church parking lot. Several people came over to greet them with enthusiastic hugs. Most of the congregants were young and dressed in jeans and t-shirts—not the traditional attire I wore when I attended church.

"This is our friend, Pam," Tony said.

The radiant joy in their eyes made me uncomfortable as they greeted me with a whole-hearted, "Welcome!"

I lowered my eyes to hide the shame of my compromised life.

We settled into our seats on the wooden pews. The stone church had high ceilings, wooden beams, and a stray dove flying overhead in the rafters.

As the service started, the beauty of the worship transported me into a peaceful place. These were not traditional hymns—they were songs from the heart of people who wanted to express their love to God.

I love you, Lord . . . and I lift my voice

To worship You, Oh, my soul rejoice!

Take joy my King in what you hear

Let it be a sweet, sweet sound in your ear

The tenderness of these angelic voices caused tears to flow, and the gentle embrace of a loving spiritual force wrapped itself around me. I trembled in humility. My parched soul softened as God's love descended. Like a thirsty flower opening to the soft, subtle rain, I lifted my head to drink in more. I had never experienced this kind of worship. The nearness of God felt tangible.

I dried my eyes as a blond-headed man in khaki pants and a blue shirt approached the microphone. I assumed he must be the pastor. As Kenn Gulliksen spoke, his words began to float around my heart like gentle music. His voice embraced me with a tenderness that made me feel loved.

I wept all over again. Tony kept peering over to see if I was okay, but I definitely wasn't. I couldn't define my encounter with this unexpected spiritual force. I tried to appear composed, but the water kept leaking from my eyes.

Kenn wasn't preaching in the traditional sense of trying to motivate people with a feel-good inspirational message. Instead, he spoke with gentleness from his heart. I envisioned Jesus standing in our midst. He spoke with wisdom not of this world. Kenn talked about God in a way that made him approachable. He didn't talk about religion but a personal relationship with a loving God. As Kenn shared about the transforming love of God, he seemed to have answers that resonated with my battered soul. *Were these the answers I needed? The answers I had been searching for? The love I longed for?*

Could this be the path I needed to find—the alternative to the one that drove me into the desert of spiritual poverty? It became evident my pain came from following what this world honors: wealth, success, power, and self-gratification. That path led me towards an empty existence. Because of my brokenness, I trusted no one, including a God I couldn't see or touch. While my shattered heart cried out for healing, my protective walls of skepticism defended against this new truth. I left my friends that day but promised to return.

Over the next few weeks, I wrestled with my doubts and reflected on my experience at the Vineyard. What's the difference between knowing *about* God and actually *knowing* Him? Is that even possible? What's the difference between the *God of the Bible* and the *Lord of my life*? I didn't understand what that meant. I prayed, but only when I ran into trouble or needed help. He became the *God of emergencies*. The rest of the time I did fine on my own. I lived life on my own terms and followed the path I thought most expedient.

I remember a conversation I had with my mother when I was nineteen years old. "Pam, you better marry before something else happens to you," referring to my two car accidents.

One nearly took my life at seventeen. On my drive to a nearby town to visit my boyfriend, I collided head-on with another car. I sustained a broken arm, a shattered right ankle, and deep lacerations inside my left cheek and on my chin. If a veterinarian hadn't stopped to help, I would have bled to death. I spent several weeks in the hospital, had two surgeries, and spent many months of recovery at home. If the cuts inside my check had been a fraction deeper, I would have had a nice scar across the outside of my face.

A year later as I drove to work, my car struck a patch of ice and spun out of control. I lifted both hands and shouted, "Jesus!" Then, miraculously, the car skidded into a ditch just yards away from a group of school kids waiting for their bus. It was a miracle they weren't hit, and I only sustained a few minor contusions.

"Mom, I'm not getting married until much later in life. I never want to say, 'If I hadn't married you, I could have . . .' I want to know when I marry it is truly what I want to do."

Even at that young age, I realized that marriage meant a big commitment. Children were a full-time responsibility. To do it right would demand more attention than I was ready to give. I wanted to experience life and realize my potential before I settled down.

I traveled this path long enough to look back on the consequences of my choices. What did I learn? Sure, there were impressive highlights that exalted my ego and fashioned a worldly persona to hide behind. But were they worth the loss of my true identity?

I experienced how the rich and famous live behind their guarded gates—often struggling with their own suspicions and uncertainties, trying to maintain their significance and manufactured images. Where there is great power and wealth, greed, lust, and exploitation abound.

Trespassing into that inner sanctum extracts a heavy admission price. It demands total allegiance to its system of avarice and imperceptibly erodes the truth with fool's gold. The playgrounds of the world are enticing and cater to the false illusions of self-aggrandizement. "What do you benefit if you gain the whole world, but lose your own soul?" (Mark 8:36 NLT).

I had no desire to repeat the painful mistakes of my past. I often thought, *Maybe I'll get it right next time. Maybe next time it'll be different.* After twenty-eight years of doing things my way, where has it gotten me? Do

I want to keep pursuing what I *think* I want? Or is it time to find out who God is?

I paced around my room. I knew I needed help, and maybe God *could* help me. What did I have to lose? My life lay in shambles, and I didn't know how to fix it. God showed up in the past with unique moments of revelation, but I never pursued them. Once the problem appeared to be solved, I'd go back to doing things my way. God sort of faded away. This time seemed different.

In my frustration, I looked up, "OK God! I want to know *if* you are real. Are you *really* who you say you are?" Then I added my conditions: "But I don't want 'churchianity' or a nice little pat on the head. I don't want to warm a pew somewhere. I have real problems and need real answers—either you've got them or you don't. Either you are who you say you are or you're not. I need to know the truth!"

Now came the ultimatum, "So, here's the deal, God—I'll give you six months. For six months, I'll take your Word literally, to the best of my ability. But I'm telling you—the first time I step out and you're not there, I'll pack my little bags, and I won't bother you anymore. I don't know where I'll go or what I'll do, but I won't bother you anymore."

God must have smiled at this audacious little girl who desperately wanted the truth. I didn't mean to be disrespectful, but I had to be honest. Trite platitudes weren't going to cut it. My gaping wounds were bleeding, and no spiritual Band-Aid would stop them.

God didn't seem offended by my challenge. No lightning bolt shot out of heaven to strike me down. If nothing is hidden from God like the Bible says, he already knows my fears, so why try and hide them? If he created me, then I doubt anything I did would surprise him. I hid from myself by reasoning and rationalizing my sin—or plain out denying it— but God knew. Maybe I didn't know how to handle my emotions, but I assumed God did.

Trust, vulnerability, and transparency were all dangerous words for me. But *if* God's love is *unconditional* . . . and *if* he will *never* leave me . . . didn't it make sense I *could* risk trusting him? Maybe I *could* be vulnerable within the safety of God's love.

"OK, God . . . you want my life? You can have it. It's not very pretty, but it's yours."

I had no religious pretense in my relationship with God. My desperation caused me to be brutally honest. If I couldn't be authentic, how could I learn to trust? Without trust, how could I ever love him completely? I had to start somewhere; I took my first step of faith. Without this honest relationship, I wouldn't have had the courage to make the hard choices, take risks, and press into the spiritual conflicts waiting around the corner.

Chapter Nine:
Taking the Plunge

COUNTING THE COST

The night is almost gone; the day of salvation will soon be here. So remove your dark deeds like dirty clothes, and put on the shining armor of right living.

Romans 13:12 NLT

Let us draw near with a sincere heart in full assurance of faith, having our hearts sprinkled clean from an evil conscience and our bodies washed with pure water.

Hebrews 10:22 NASB

T he Vineyard became the first church that felt like home, and Sundays were a day of joyous celebration. The services were brimming with youthful exuberance, creativity, and the powerful presence of God. People from all walks of life, including the entertainment industry, attended. Worshiping together and being taught the Word of God forged eternal bonds and created a beautiful spiritual family. The sweet presence of God descended and brought revitalizing refreshment.

The Daisy, a Christian nightclub where musicians performed in a non-alcoholic environment, was turned into the Vineyard School of Discipleship for three-months during the day. Since I told God I'd take his Word literally for six months, I figured I'd better find out what it said.

The pastors taught from their expertise on pivotal books of the Bible. The depth of the Word revealed a God I never understood. The more I learned, the more fascinated I became. We were going to the school of the Holy Spirit and learning new life skills from a Biblical perspective.

There were twenty-five to thirty students, and it became an accelerated time of spiritual growth. Senior pastor and Vineyard founder, Kenn Gulliksen, taught my favorite class on "The Principles of Discipleship."

Kenn, a highly respected and gifted teacher, had a gentle way of unlocking the wisdom of Scripture. He made the biblical principles relevant and practical. During one of our classes, Kenn suggested we pray for what God placed on our hearts. He led the prayer and then opened it to the rest of the class. One by one, different students prayed, including me.

After Kenn closed in prayer and everyone returned to rustling papers, preparing for the next lesson, Kenn made an unusual comment. "We all have our own way of praying," he said. "I pray like the New American Standard Bible, and Pam prays like the Amplified Bible." Everyone laughed . . . except me.

That comment utterly mortified me, and my face flushed with embarrassment. The Amplified Bible expanded the text and used more words than traditional Bibles. My self-esteem, still in need of repair, took it as a chastisement and failed to see the humor. What he intended as a playful comment devastated me.

As my head hung over my open Bible, big drops plopped onto the pages. The sound of my tears hitting the tissue-thin paper resounded so loudly in my mind, I imagined everyone in the room could hear them. I couldn't look at anyone because I thought they were making fun of me for talking too much in prayer.

Kenn suggested a fifteen-minute break before returning to class. I slipped out the side door to avoid any interactions with the students. I had to decide if I wanted to race home in humiliation or find the courage to return to class. The tears wouldn't stop flowing as I stared at the sky, wondering what to do. A verse came to mind: "Give thanks in all circumstances, for this is God's will for you in Christ Jesus" (1 Thessalonians 5:18).

Give thanks in all circumstances? Really? I wiped the snot dripping from my nose.

"OK, let's see," I half-heartedly lifted my hands and said a feeble prayer, "Praise you, Jesus," then cried even harder.

This is insane, sneered a negative voice inside my head.

I tried again, choking back tears, "Praise you, Jesus."

If anyone saw you out here, they'd think you were a complete idiot, chided that cynical voice again. *What are you praising God for when you're hurting and have tears running down your face? This is absurd!*

I wasn't making much headway in the reasoning department.

"Lord, your Word says to praise you in all things, not necessarily for all things." I tried to refute the negative thoughts. Still fearful of how ridiculous I might look, I tried again. "Praise you, Jesus!" Each declaration of praise became stronger with practice.

Walking back to the classroom, the pain lifted, my tears dried, and I sensed a gentle peace by the time I reached the door. As everyone took their seats, I took mine with a renewed sense of relief.

What just happened? Where did that pain come from? Kenn made an innocuous little comment. Why did it strike such a deep chord inside me? The Bible says God inhabits the praises of his people (Psalm 22:3 KJV). Even as weak as mine were, he honored my effort to praise him amid my humiliation and tears.

As I continued to learn the fundamentals of my new faith, I realized I needed spiritual cleansing in the waters of baptism and had to be "born of water."

My parents had me sprinkled with water when they dedicated me as a baby, but I learned that total immersion symbolized the death, burial, and resurrection of Jesus. Being immersed in the water meant choosing to identify, symbolically, with the "death" of Jesus and my former life. The old life is "buried" with Christ and washed away, and my new life emerges in "resurrection" power.

Do you not know that all of us who have been baptized into Christ Jesus were baptized into his death? We were buried therefore with him by baptism into death, in order that, just as Christ was raised from the dead by the glory of the Father, we too might walk in the newness of life. For if we have been united with him in a death like his, we shall certainly be united with him in a resurrection like his. (Romans 6:3–5, ESV)

The Vineyard planned a baptism celebration at Santa Monica's beach. Being baptized in the Pacific Ocean sounded exciting.

My white gauzy top and pants covered my bikini and the thin gold chain around my size-two waist. When I took off my outer garments to prepare for baptism, I realized my tiny bikini barely covered my body. The gentle persuasion of the Holy Spirit made me uncomfortable with my near-nakedness. I never owned a one-piece suit, but I sure could have used one now. I quickly grabbed my top and covered myself. Modesty had returned to my life.

The sun warmed me as I sat on the beach and sang worship songs under a white canopy of puffy clouds. I marveled at the magnitude of God's handiwork while the breeze danced playfully across the ocean. With my toes dug into the sand, I contemplated the importance of my commitment.

"OK, Lord," I whispered, "I am doing this in obedience to your Word. Today I will bury my old life and wash it out to sea. If I never stand in front of a camera or do anything in Hollywood again . . . I will live the life *you* created for me. Today starts my new life with you."

Two pastors held me firmly on either side and plunged me under the water. I rose to soft praises surrounding me—clean and free.

Kenn Gulliksen, Founder, Vineyard Christian Fellowship

Keith Green and Kenn

Keith, Jerry Houser, and Kenn baptizing in Santa Monica

My friend Doug and I drove to the Santa Monica Pier for coffee before heading home. We ordered from a small stand on the pier. I turned and nearly knocked over a disheveled young boy standing behind me. He looked about twelve.

"I am sorry," I said. The boy didn't move. He stood there and stared at me.

"Are you hungry?"

Yes, he nodded.

I ordered him a hamburger, fries, and a hot chocolate. We moved to a table, and I said, "What's your name?"

"Ray." We sat with him while he ate.

"What are you doing here, Ray?"

"I ran away from a group home, and I have a bed under the pier."

The thought of a child sleeping in such vulnerable circumstances shocked me. We tried to figure out what we could do for him. Doug worked all day, and I lived alone, but we couldn't let him stay here.

"There's a Christian crisis house in Hollywood that just opened," Doug said, "I think it's called Centrum. Would you like to go there, Ray?"

"They won't turn me in, will they?" He stiffened at the thought.

"I don't think so, but I know they will help you."

Doug called and let them know we were coming.

I stared out the window of the car as we neared the house. Hollywood resembled desolation row with its crumbling, rundown buildings, XXX shops, and the odd assortment of characters wandering the streets.

"The city plans to restore this neighborhood and make it a tourist attraction," Doug said, "Right now, this is where the runaway kids hang out and sleep in the squats."

"Squats?" I said.

"The abandoned buildings waiting to be torn down. There are also a lot of working girls around here."

Right off the main strip of Hollywood Boulevard on Sycamore Street stood a once beautiful, now dilapidated, two-story house. Its peeled paint and sagging porch steps suggested years of neglect. We walked into what reminded me of a musty thrift store with mismatched furniture and worn-out rugs. As I took in this strange environment, laughter erupted from around the corner. I ventured in and encountered a diverse group seated around a dinner table.

"Welcome!" Tim, the house manager, said. "Come in. Want something to eat?"

"No, thank you. We've already eaten."

I knew nothing about mission work except for the missionaries who went to Africa or a Third World country. But here, in the heart of Hollywood, existed a new kind of mission field. Despite the ramshackle conditions, a warm lightness caressed me.

I'd never witnessed God reaching out to the needs of people in such a practical way. After bringing Ray to Centrum, I followed up with him while getting to know the staff.

The house only took men. When women came seeking help, I found myself volunteering to take them to my apartment. My one-bedroom apartment soon became overrun with two girls in my king-size bed, another on the couch in the den, and me on the couch in my living room. The women stayed at the men's house during the day for Bible studies, meals, and activities.

I began to envision a bigger house for more girls. I thought how fun it would be. *We can hang chintz curtains, bake bread, and Jesus can heal everyone.* But rents were too expensive, and it was only a dream anyway.

"How you doing, Pam?" Kleg Seth, the founder of Centrum said. "You doing OK? Any problems with the girls?"

"No, so far, so good," I said to the lanky Lutheran pastor looking down at me with his smiling eyes.

"You know you can call me day or night if you need anything." Kleg's dedication inspired me. "I know how difficult this can be. You're doing a great job, and I appreciate your help."

"Thanks, Kleg. I don't know how you do it. You're always so calm. When do you sleep?"

He laughed and shook his well-groomed head of red hair. "It's the grace of God that keeps me going." The man worked tirelessly without complaint. The staff drew strength from his stability.

"Pam, we want to open a women's house, and since you've been working with the women, would you consider being the director?"

"Me?" My mouth dropped open. It's one thing to daydream, but another thing when it becomes a reality.

"Yes, we want to rent a house on the next street over for women."

This meant giving up my apartment and living in the house with the girls. "Can I pray about this?" This had to be God because I knew I couldn't handle the position.

I hadn't even finished the three-month course at the School of Discipleship. Now, they want me to run a crisis house dealing with at-risk youth, prostitutes, and all the other indigents in need. How crazy is this?

I cornered several of the pastors at school. "What do you think of me being the director of Centrum's new women's home?"

They were supposed to say, "Pam, you are not qualified." Instead, they said, "Pam, you'd be great!"

Inside my head I cried, *What? I'm too young to die!* This move meant death to my independence and way of life.

I went to my senior pastor, Kenn Gulliksen, for confirmation. I mustered the nerve to ask, "What do you think? About me directing the women's house in Hollywood?"

Our eyes locked, and tears welled up. There, peering straight into my soul, were the smiling eyes of Jesus. As impossible as it sounds, the supernatural eyes of Jesus looked directly at me through my pastor.

"Pick up your cross and follow Jesus," he said, drawing from Matthew 16:24–26.

As much as I didn't want to hear those words, I knew Jesus spoke through Kenn. I dissolved into the chair. This should have been the final confirmation I needed, but I still wavered in my decision.

That weekend every time I tried to pray; my thoughts distracted me.

"I need to go shopping."

"No, I'll go swimming."

My mind couldn't focus. When I thought about the house, I felt Jesus said, "Get down on your knees and count the cost. This is not a game." *Get down on my knees! Game? Who thought this was a game? Count the cost? What cost?*

"'For which of you, intending to build a tower, does not sit down first and count the cost?'" (Luke 14:28 NKJV).

This decision involved a giant leap of faith. I had an image of myself crawling to the edge of the Grand Canyon. I peered over, and the sight of the bottomless abyss made me dizzy. If I step off this ledge, I'll be obliterated with no chance of survival. It would be tantamount to suicide. There is no way I'll make it to the other side.

Yet, that's what Jesus asked me to do—step out in faith with no safety net and walk on thin air. More than terrifying, this is insane!

"I don't know these people," I whined, "I don't know if I want to know these people. God, I don't know what I am doing." I lived a life of selfish indulgence. Yes, I wanted to know God, but I didn't believe I could do this.

If I gave my life to Jesus, I feared he would send me to some remote country with people I couldn't relate to. Instead, he found a mission field right here in Hollywood. Yet, when I thought about it, he had already started to work in my heart. Didn't I have several girls living with me? Didn't I want a bigger apartment? Hadn't my heart gone out to them?

I threw my hands in the air and said, "Fine, if you want to use this life, OK. It's yours. But it will be *you* doing it through me because I have no idea what I am doing."

I thought I heard God say with a grin, *Good. Because then I'll get all the glory.*

I laughed and said, "You've got that right. You sure will."

What did I know about God? I had so much to learn. It would only be through him that I could have any impact on these damaged lives. Despite the many confirmations I received, I looked for more. My flesh fought to hang on to its last remnants of control. I laid on my couch, wrestling with God, and hit upon an "aha" moment.

"OK, what about this? The School of Discipleship taught me that *you* give us the peace that surpasses all understanding when *you* confirm what you're doing. Well, I have no peace, so this can't be you!"

I had a moment of smugness, thinking I had outsmarted God.

It's unclear how long I lay there. It might have been a minute or maybe an hour before I lifted my head and said, "Wait a minute? Wasn't there a near-hysterical girl here just a minute ago?" I had the peace that surpassed all understanding.

I couldn't even freak out about the fact I had the supernatural peace of God. I laid my head back down and slept better than I had in weeks.

If God had a purpose for my life, I wanted to find it. Isn't that what I prayed for when I received water baptism? Didn't I pray, "I will live the life *you* created me for? Today starts my new life with you." I guess this is it. Not really what I expected.

This became the final confirmation I needed to accept his leading into the most incredible adventure of my life. I had nothing left to wrestle against. I just needed to let Kleg know I decided to accept his offer as director of the women's house.

Yes, I stepped off the edge. I looked up to Jesus, took a deep breath and said, like Esther said in the Old Testament, "If I die, I die."

As I stepped off that cliff onto the thin air, an astonishing thing happened. I stepped right into the palm of God's hand. While I couldn't see anything except my ultimate doom, God's hand became visible once I took a step of faith and carried me to the other side. "Faith is the substance of things hoped for, the evidence of things not seen" (Hebrews11:1 NKJV).

Chapter Ten:
Kingdom Madness

OLD FEARS VS. NEW TRUTH

For my thoughts are not your thoughts,
neither are your ways my ways, declares the LORD.
As the heavens are higher than the earth,
so are my ways higher than your ways
and my thoughts than your thoughts.

Isaiah 55:8-9

I enjoyed spending time at the men's house and attended some of their Bible studies. Since the women spent their days at the house, I usually picked them up after dinner before bringing them back to my apartment. The house bustled with activity, and the girls helped with the cleaning and food preparations until the women's house became available. There were always interesting conversations to glean from.

I didn't know much about what some called their "heavenly language" or the gift of "speaking in tongues." When the two leaders started discussing it, I became intrigued.

"I don't know why it is so difficult for people to understand such a beautiful gift from God," Tim said. "It's like how a child learns to speak. He makes sounds and moves his lips."

"Yes, but then the devil will say, 'that's stupid and you're foolish,'" his friend said.

Tim laughed. "That's what the devil wants you to think, but he's a liar. He'll do anything to stop that power gift."

"Yeah," said his friend, "but our intellect and pride get in the way. It's hard to do what you don't understand."

"For sure, that's another barrier the enemy puts up," Tim said. "We want to be 'in control' and we 'need to know,' but that's not faith. If you release the Spirit's flow, *your* spirit grows stronger."

93

I turned the page of the magazine I was pretending to read as I continued to listen.

"What does a baby say? Dada or mama . . . those are usually the first words they babble until learning to put sentences together."

Hmm, I thought. *That makes sense. I never heard it shared that way.*

That night, I thought about the conversation as I climbed into bed. Under the cover of darkness, I tried it.

"Ah, baa, daa, do."

This is stupid. How ludicrous is this? Wait! Isn't that what the enemy would say?

OK, let's try this again: "Daa, boo, dee, maa." This time I giggled under the covers. I felt foolish. How silly. This is what they said would happen. After a few more baby babblings were uttered, I chuckled to myself before I fell asleep. It made little sense, but then they said it wouldn't. Could I call my babbling a heavenly language?

A few weeks later, Keith Green presented a concert at church. He was not only a gifted musician but also a charismatic evangelist with a contagious passion for Jesus. Toward the end of his concert, he talked about the baptism of the Holy Spirit and extended an invitation to come forward for prayer. Not sure my babbling qualified; I went forward for an official baptism in the Holy Spirit. My eyes moistened as the tender presence of Jesus overwhelmed me, and I released my new prayer language.

A few days later, I received a surprise phone call from my former acting agent. "I have an audition for you, Pam—it's for a small part on the TV show *Wonder Woman.*"

"OK," I responded out of habit without thinking, and took the information for the audition. But, I swear, as soon as I hung up the phone, Satan reached his boney hand through the phone and grabbed me by the throat as fear tied a knot in my stomach. *Why is this happening now? Why did I agree to this audition?* I no longer had any intention of pursuing a career in the business.

Hollywood is more about rejection than acceptance. You can go on fifty auditions, and you're lucky if you get one offer. "No, thank you," is the typical response, "but we'll keep you in mind for next time." Unfortunately, I didn't have the resilience to keep putting myself through that disappointment.

I faced my share of rejection and the sting of not being good enough. Over time, that leaks into your belief system. Not being right for something differs from not being good enough—a distinction I had a hard time making. For actors, or any creative person, self-worth can become invested in performance, and if it's rejected or criticized, it feels like a personal attack. I loved the creativity, but the process dented my confidence.

As the audition drew near, I panicked. *Why didn't I say no?* The need to pray in my prayer language overtook me. *What do I have to lose?* I paced around my apartment and poured my emotions into this unknown language. I didn't understand a word I said. The fear of the audition replaced my self-consciousness about speaking in a heavenly language or whatever this was ". . . but the Spirit is here to help us. For example, when we don't know what to pray for, the Spirit prays for us in ways that cannot be put into words" (Romans 8:26 CEV).

This audition seemed like an attempt by Satan to lure me back into his lair to be judged, scrutinized, and rejected. All my past fears resurfaced, and for the next few days, I continued to pray in my prayer language.

On the day of the audition, I drove to the Warner Brothers Studios and made my way to the casting director's office. Each step gave me greater peace. A childlike curiosity insulated me as I sat in the waiting area, detached from the surrounding activity. A producer walked by and asked, "Are you here for an audition?"

"I am."

"Would you mind stepping into my office for a minute?"

"Sure." There wasn't an ounce of fear as we chatted. Instead, my genuine interest in his life seemed to disarm him.

He thanked me and said, "It was nice talking with you. Good luck on your audition." I went back to the seating area and waited to be called.

"Pamela Rice," said the woman with the clipboard.

"Yes, that's me." I rose to enter the room behind her. I stood in the middle of the sizable room, and my eyes scanned the room, taking note of the production staff. The casting director examined me from behind his sleek executive desk, and four other people sat with clipboards to his left. That same childlike curiosity insulated me from this room full of scrutinizing eyes. When I returned their gaze, they could not look me in the eye. I sensed hazy darkness encircling them, but I didn't feel afraid. In fact, it fascinated me to watch each one lower their eyes.

The casting director motioned me over to sit as he explained the role. We read the script through.

"Is that it?" I said as I turned the page over.

"Yes, I am sorry." He seemed embarrassed. "It's just a few lines."

"That's OK. I didn't want to miss anything."

After reading the lines again, I thanked them and headed for the door.

A rush of victory flooded me as I walked to my car—I did it!

That night, as I processed the experience, it dawned on me, the power of my prayer language replaced my anxiety with a childlike curiosity. But it still surprised me when the next day my agent called. "Congratulations! You got the part."

I played the secretary at a corrupt music company where Wonder Woman, Lynda Carter, comes to meet with my boss, and we have a short exchange.

My prayer language became my new best friend. I continued praying the day of the shoot. As I left the makeup trailer, I met Lynda, and we strolled to the set making idle chitchat. The director went over his last-minute instructions, and we shot the scene in one take. Just one take and done. Lynda and a few crew members thanked me, and I left the set.

I couldn't have planned a more perfect ending to this chapter of my life. Walking away from the industry having conquered the intimidation it caused me in the past made me feel like a victorious warrior. I felt like David must have when he slew Goliath. Whenever I didn't know how to pray (and there were many), I prayed in tongues. His Spirit strengthened my Spirit and revealed insights into God's ways. Finally, I understood why Paul professed in 1 Corinthians 14:

> For anyone who speaks in a tongue does not speak to people but to God. . . . Anyone who speaks in a tongue edifies themselves. . . . I would like every one of you to speak in tongues. . . .I thank God that I speak in tongues more than all of you. (vv. 2, 4, 5, 18)

Chapter Eleven:
Heel Marks to the Cross

I'M TOO YOUNG TO DIE

. . . but your Father already knows your needs. Seek the Kingdom of God above all else, and he will give you everything you need.

Luke 12:30-31 NLT

Time to move! The crisis house that Centrum rented belonged to a former cult, and when the city permits for the "renovations" to the neighborhood received approval, they planned to demolish it and our provisional lease would end. Not a situation that provided a sense of security.

All the confirmations I received did not make my move any easier. I dug my heels into the ground as the Lord drew me into his will. I am ashamed to say I left deep heel marks to the cross. Yes, I wanted to know the truth. I wanted to know God, but my heart throbbed with fear. My flesh, more potent than I thought, waged a battle that can still occasionally rear its ugly head. There will always be a choice between my will and God's will. But every time I answer "yes" to Jesus, I gain new freedom despite my fears.

I spent the first night in the house alone. Why I did remains unclear. The brisk night air made its way through the broken windows of the abandoned house. I wrapped my sweater around me and looked for the door locks. There were none. No heat—no running water—no locks. *What am I doing here?*

As I lay in the upstairs bedroom, eyes wide open, unable to sleep, the sound of a muffled "pop" caused me to stiffen. Two more "pops" followed. Were those gunshots? *Oh, my God in heaven, what have I done?* I grabbed my Bible and clenched it to my chest as I lay there, wondering if I would live or die. The gunshots ceased once the police sirens came blaring down the boulevard. Then a brief silence before the sound of bottles breaking and a garbage can rattling down the alley. The muffled altercations sounded like men fighting.

Oh, God. This can't be you, my mind insisted. *This can't be your will.* I grappled with these thoughts, glued to my bed, afraid to move.

I dozed off as dawn washed away the terror of the night. I woke, my body still tense but thankful for the familiar voices downstairs. I dragged myself into the kitchen.

Kleg greeted me with a cheerful "How did you sleep?"

"How did I sleep? Who can sleep with gunshots going off, sirens blasting, and fights in the alley?"

"You'll get used to it." Kleg laughed.

I wasn't sure I wanted to!

A team from church came to start the house repairs, and Kleg made arrangements to send two male staff to sleep downstairs every night until the house became secure.

I saw the house as a symbol of God's transformative love. Life had used, abused, and neglected this once beautiful house, much like the women who would live here. But with some tender loving care, I hoped they would both be restored and find new life.

I wanted to create a home environment for the women, not a stark, whitewashed ministry with everyone crammed into metal bunk beds. These women needed the warmth of a home to remind them of what life could be like with love. The house became a flurry of activity as volunteers showed up to help paint the bedrooms and refinish the hardwood floors. Some wonderful ladies from the church came to hang curtains and add bedspreads to finish the newly painted rooms. Each room received a different color paint and had its own unique style.

Word hit the street we were open and our home soon filled with new guests. I managed the primary responsibilities, organized the schedules, taught Bible studies, and did my best to resolve conflicts. Every night I collapsed into bed, wondering if what I did mattered to anyone.

Passing through the kitchen, I heard the girls talking outside on the back porch.

"Who does she think she is?"

What? A tirade of thoughts flooded my mind, *Who do I think I am? How dare they!*

Their words pierced me. *I am doing everything I can to help these women, and this is the thanks I get?* My pride, once pricked, didn't do well.

I vented my frustration to God. He didn't chide me but whispered, "Remember how skeptical you were and how difficult it still is for you to trust?" His gentle touch soothed my injured ego. "I know your heart. I see your efforts." I knew it was God's comfort speaking since those thoughts were foreign to my own.

I didn't need to earn their approval. God's approval mattered the most. So, I humbled my pride and asked God to forgive me, "As iron sharpens iron[3], so one man sharpens another."

The ministry reminded me of a hothouse that grows extraordinary plants under extreme conditions. The daily pressures of ministry exposed my weaknesses, and I learned to surrender them to Jesus. God used these women to bring healing into my life just as much as he used me to bring healing into theirs.

Serving these women shaped me as a Christian. They demanded selfless love—not just empty words. Every day a part of *me* died to make way for more of Jesus.

When I asked the Lord to give me a better understanding of how to help these women, a vision unfolded during prayer. I saw myself sitting on a large boulder overlooking a sandy beach with gentle waves lapping the shore. The open beachfront extended some distance from the water up to a dense, jungle-like forest. I sat silently on this rock and knew it was vital for me to be still.

Wounded animals emerged from the dark forest. These severely maimed animals—one by one—came out onto the shore. They were desperate for the water but fearful of exposure on the open beachfront. Any sudden move would send them rushing back to the forest. It grieved me to see these injured animals. One hobbled out with a back leg chewed off, and another's back was slashed to the bone. The blood from their wounds matted and mingled with the dirt in their fur. Crouched over, searching right and left, they made their way across the open sand in search of water, ready to bolt at any movement.

I sat quietly on the rock observing their tenuous behaviors as tears blurred my eyes. The Lord painted a metaphor. Although, their wounds were not visible, these women were deeply wounded like the animals in my vision. They hid in the darkness but thirsted for the water. The Word of God is often described as the living water of eternal life. If they overcame their fears and made it to the water, they would find relief. But if they were startled, they would attack or run back into the darkness.

My eyes opened to the spiritual reality of the situation, and a part of God's compassion penetrated my heart. What these damaged women said—their insults, stubbornness, and rebellion—was only a defense. Trusting anyone and exposing their true selves made them vulnerable and at risk for being hurt.

I understood because I saw a part of my own heart reflected in them. Maybe not to the same degree, but enough to know I had my own walls of self protection from vulnerability. This vision shifted my perspective, and I looked beyond the obvious for the need that created it. I wanted eyes to see the hidden person of the heart, and that required a gentle and quiet spirit like Peter expressed in 1 Peter 3:4.

Chapter Twelve:
A Journey of Compassion

DAMAGED BEYOND REPAIR?

The LORD is near to the brokenhearted
and saves those who are crushed in spirit

Psalm 34:18

"Pam, it's nice you want to help people," my mother said, "But how are you going to live without a salary?" She didn't understand this extreme change of direction. I didn't fully understand it myself.

"Ed sends me a little money each month, and the ministry takes care of my food and rent." I tried to ease her concerns. "If God sent me here, then it's up to him to provide for me, isn't it?" My mother didn't always agree with my life choices, but she didn't try to control me. As long as I was happy, she was happy. She didn't know about everything I went through. My father, on the other hand, understood the importance of my need to experience the adventure of life and explore my capabilities.

H.F., my dear friend and confidant, didn't know what to think. He thought of my decision as a passing phase. "Do what you need to do, Pam," he said, "when you're ready you can always come back here." I don't think he expected me to last more than six months.

Living in the house stripped away all the materialistic façades, exposing the raw realities of life. The devastating effects of poverty and abuse brought to mind the ruins of a battlefield. Those who survived the hardships in their life were the walking wounded. The sight of these wounded lives became unbearable at times. In those moments, I wanted to retreat to my former self-indulgent lifestyle, forgetting the pain of the past and only remembering the more refined creature comforts.

I better understood why the Hebrews wanted to return to Egypt. They forgot about the slave pit and only remembered their meals of meat and fish. I experienced what the world had to offer and knew it would not bring me fulfillment, so no matter how challenging my pursuit of God became, there would be no turning back.

I sat with Jenny, a nineteen-year-old prostitute blanketed by the sun's soothing warmth on the back porch. Jenny wanted to escape her "boyfriend," who was her pimp and his violent assaults. A gentle peace surrounded us as Jenny opened up about her life. Her big brown eyes blinked with an unnatural frequency, betraying her dark history before she even spoke.

"My dad did things to me as a kid. He said if I didn't do what he wanted, he'd pound the s— out of me." She casually puffed on her cigarette. "And he did . . . lots of times."

I sat motionless as she continued.

"When he got drunk, he made me dance for his friends . . . They passed me around." The emptiness in her voice revealed her resignation. I couldn't imagine such exploitation.

"If I cried, he would beat me with his belt."

The thought of a father who could do this to his child disgusted me. "How old were you?"

"With my dad? Ten."

I felt nauseous. "Jenny, I am so sorry." I turned my head away and tried not to embarrass her with my tears. I'd never heard such a story.

"I tried to kill myself a few times. They should have let me die, but they took me to some Seventh-Day Adventist hospital and gave me shock treatments."

The unnatural blinking of her eyes became part of the permanent damage from those inhumane treatments. No wonder this young girl thought she was nothing more than a piece of meat for men to devour.

I looked up into the comforting blue sky and brushed away my tears. I realized no human source had the power necessary to heal Jenny's damaged life: no doctor, no drug, no husband, no self-help book. She needed the healing balm of God's love. Only God could restore what they brutally ripped away from her.

But how?

How do you restore a life tossed, like a piece of refuse, into the sewers of life? How could I help her believe in the power of love when all she knew was abuse? I wanted to hold her in my arms and rock her until all her pain disappeared. *Jesus, have mercy on this child. Help me reach her with your love.*

As God exposed the motives of my heart, I learned to repent. When he tore down the false façade of my self-sufficiency, I became dependent on his goodness. The more I embedded his Word in my heart, the clearer my spiritual vision became. Jesus knew the hearts of men because there was no guile within him. He had no ulterior motive but the Father's will. As I continued to yield my life to the Lordship of Jesus, he continued to cleanse my heart, and his power flowed more freely through me. The unseen battle with the forces of darkness became clearer.

God came to heal, restore, and redeem, and the evil one came to kill, rob, steal and destroy. I witnessed his devastating handiwork in the lives surrounding me every day. But, amid the devastation, the loving compassion of Jesus offered living water to these parched souls. Even in my bewilderment, I never took my eyes off the one who came to save these lives from the grip of the enemy.

His love magnetized me. If I took my eyes off Jesus, I would have only seen despair. Instead, I followed him as he searched for the lost. God showed me his unconditional love for humanity and revealed his heart of mercy. I kept pressing into his Word for more answers.

During prayer, I had a picture of me as a toddler, standing before Jesus, who loomed, enormous, towering over the land. He wore the white robes and sandals pictured in the children's Sunday school stories. As Jesus walked through the countryside over mountains and through valleys, I desperately wanted to follow him, but his colossal footsteps covered too vast a distance. My little feet scurried as fast as they could behind him. Determined to keep up with him, I grabbed hold of the hem of his garment. My tiny feet lifted off the ground, and I was blowing in the wind, soaring through the sky and hanging on for dear life.

No metaphor could be more apt for this season of my life.

Chapter Thirteen:
The Pain of Tarnished Souls

IF JESUS CAN'T HELP ME, NO ONE CAN

"The LORD doesn't see things the way you see them. People judge by outward appearance, but the LORD looks at the heart."

1 Samuel 16:7 NLT

K leg phoned from the men's house. "Do you have time to interview a new girl?"

"Sure, where is she?"

"She's in your living room," he responded.

I headed downstairs and, after a quick walk through the house, called Kleg back.

"There's no one here. Do you think she left?" It wasn't unusual for new girls to have second thoughts. "There's a guy here I haven't seen before. Should I send him over to the men's house?"

"No, Pam, that boy is a girl. She came into the house identifying as a male, and for three days, we thought she was Victor. Today she told me her real name is Victoria."

"Really?" I held my breath while fear crept up the back of my neck.

Kleg must have sensed the stress in my voice, "I'll be right over, and we can interview her together."

I bolted upstairs, "No way, God! You have gone too far this time. I can't handle this . . . No way!" I slammed my bedroom door. "I'm going to the Bahamas!"

How could I allow this woman, who identified as a man, into this house filled with women? I already had a difficult time managing their needs, but this pushed me beyond my limits. Why did God put me in such impossible situations?

When Kleg arrived, I reluctantly descended the stairs. Sure enough, there sat the Mexican boy I passed in the living room. I understood how she easily fooled the staff at the men's house. Her short haircut, damaged teeth, oversized work shirt, and straight-legged black pants obscured any evidence of a woman. Even the DMV identified her as "Victor Mendoza."

Victoria sat with her hands folded, staring at the floor. I couldn't imagine admitting her into the house. Putting her in an intimate setting with vulnerable women would be like putting a kid in a candy store.

"Why do you want to be a part of this house?" I said.

"If Jesus can't help me, no one can," she said as a tear slid down the side of her cheek.

Wasn't this why we started the house? Was there anyone beyond God's healing power? How could I turn her away?

I assigned her to a room across from mine.

"Why does she get a room by herself?" others asked. I couldn't tell them I wanted to protect them. I had no idea how to handle the depth of her issues.

Our crisis house allowed women a thirty-day stay to meet their immediate needs. At the end of their stay, they were offered placement in a long-term discipleship program through other ministries in the area. I sent Vicky to several long-term programs, but she continued to end up back on our doorstep. I confess, much to my shame, that my heart sank each time I pulled into the driveway and found her sitting on the back porch. But the more time I spent with Vicky, the more I grew to appreciate her and the blessing she became.

The daily personality clashes, lying, stealing, breaking of rules, and hostile attitudes between the women challenged every nerve in my body. Vicky became my undercover agent and collected information that gave me insight into these complex situations. Her street savvy cut through their manipulations and helped me mediate discipline.

Vicky enjoyed taking on routine chores around the house, but her charismatic personality could turn into a bully when I wasn't around. I took a phone call after dinner and left the girls to clean the kitchen. When I returned, Vicky and another girl were arguing.

"What right does she have to tell me what to do?" she said. "She doesn't run this house."

I stepped in and pulled Vicky aside, "I know you want to help, and I appreciate your efforts, but you can't boss the girls around. I've warned you before, and next time I'll have to ask you to leave."

Vicky hung her head, "I'm sorry. I won't do it again."

As she stood in front of me, I saw an image of fragmented body parts superimposed over her, like Frankenstein with all his different body parts sewn together with stitches to form a human likeness. Vicky's heart looked similar. Broken pieces of her heart were stitched together haphazardly and covered with filthy Band-Aids.

Is that what a human heart looks like when trying to survive abuse? I better understood why God says, "I will give you a new heart . . ." Who can live with such gross distortions? A wave of compassion swept over me as I tried to imagine what she must have experienced.

Occasionally I caught a glimpse of the little girl behind her tough exterior. As we sat chatting in my office, I asked, "Vicky, where is your mother?"

Her smile disappeared, and the iron gate of protection slammed shut. "I don't want to talk about her."

"OK, I get it. I only wanted to know if you had family."

"No, I have none, and I don't want none." She became agitated.

"I'm sorry."

"Why? My mother was a lousy drunk and a drug addict." I sat quietly and listened as she continued. "She thought it was cute to sit me on top of the bar while men bought her drinks. She'd take them home, tie me to the end of the bed, and have sex with them. She was a f***ing whore." Her face flushed, and perspiration appeared on her forehead.

"Vicky, that's horrible."

"Yeah, I hated those men, and if I said anything, she beat the crap out of me. When I got big enough, I fought back and landed in juvenile hall."

"If you hated men . . . why did you dress like one?"

"I fell in love with a woman who had a kid." Vicky chuckled. "She was straight, and I wanted to protect them from any gossip or judgment."

After becoming a transvestite (dressing and acting like a man), she married a transvestite man. **Their marriage consisted of a man and a woman only their roles were reversed.**

It might be easy to assume Vicky was a transgender woman in today's culture since she lived as "Victor" and married a transgender man. But her gender identity was more complex. She entered our women's house and identified herself as a woman using the feminine form of her name, "Victoria."

After many conversations, Vicky shared how she became a drug dealer and overdosed on amphetamines before graduating to the harder drug heroin. She'd been arrested multiple times as an East Los Angeles gangster and served five years in prison for manslaughter after killing a policeman in a drug bust.

"They wouldn't let me into the general population but kept me in the bull pen."

"What's that?" I'd never heard of such a thing.

"It's a special section in prison to keep us 'bull dykes' away from the women." My throat constricted when she labeled herself in graphic street terms. Her history didn't reflect my experience with the person who sat in front of me. I changed the subject.

"So, tell me Vicky, why did you get that big shrunken head tattoo on your forearm?"

"It sent a message. Shut your mouth, or you're dead." My stomach started to knot up with fear. The little girl disappeared, and the darkness of her soul emerged.

The powerful truth of Vicky's words, "If Jesus can't help me, no one can," rang in my ears.

Kleg called an emergency staff meeting to inform us he received a phone call from a correctional officer at Sybil Brand, "He asked if we would take temporary custody of one of their teenage girls. They want to release her pending sentencing, but she has no place to go. I'm going to pick her up. We'll be back in time for dinner."

He returned with a frail, blond sixteen-year-old named Janet. She sat politely at the dinner table, but her eyes conveyed mistrust. After showing her to her room, I went downstairs to the kitchen to talk with Kleg.

"What did she do?" I wanted to know since Sybil Brand was a women's prison.

"They accused her of manslaughter," Kleg said, as he reached for the coffeepot. "She shot a man, and the bullet is still lodged in his head."

I sank into the chair. "That little girl shot a man?"

Kleg poured a cup of coffee, "Yes, and if he dies within the year, the charge will be first-degree murder. No one wants to touch this."

"Where's her family?"

"They aren't interested in helping her." Kleg sipped his coffee and then added, "That's why she's here."

"What are we going to do?"

"I don't know. Let's ask God to show us."

We joined hands and asked God for his wisdom. These situations were beyond my comprehension.

Vicky gained Janet's confidence and discovered what really happened. Janet gave Vicky the names of people that might confirm her story.

Vicky and I drove to the neighborhood to follow up, hoping to find someone willing to help her. The media gave the area a reputation in the 80s for unsolved crimes, gang wars, and routine violence. It was predominantly African American during the crack-cocaine epidemic.

I whispered, "Jesus, Jesus, Jesus," under my breath, feeling vulnerable in a place I didn't belong.

I parked my little red Volkswagen and wondered aloud if the three rough-looking men sitting on the porch across the street knew where Janet lived. Vicky decided to find out and marched over to them as I sat in the car. After a few minutes, one of them pointed to a house down the street. Vicky returned, "Her family lives over there."

I knocked on the door. The woman who answered eyed us up and down before she allowed us to enter. The disheveled living room smelled of rancid cooking oil and a plate of half-eaten food sat on the coffee table. The oversized woman with greying black hair turned out to be Janet's mother. She told me, "Janet has always been in trouble. She does what she wants, and no one can control her." She never asked me any questions about her daughter and seemed evasive about the circumstances surrounding her arrest.

I spoke to the next-door neighbor and discovered that the man Janet shot worked as the local drug dealer. His buyers scapegoated Janet to protect their supplier. He had forced himself on her sexually when she was high on PCP; she grabbed his gun to defend herself, and it went off, shooting him in the head. That confirmed Janet's story, but no one would back her up in court. They were too afraid of the consequences; historically, the criminal justice system has not treated African Americans with equity.

I doubt they would have tolerated me, a little white girl, in their neighborhood—let alone talked with me—if Vicky hadn't been with me. She looked tough enough to demand their respect. Without her, I never would have ventured into the heart of Black Los Angeles to gather the information needed to help Janet.

"Kleg, we can't let Janet get sent to jail," I said after explaining what we learned.

"She defended herself and got set up." The injustice infuriated me. "I'm going to petition the judge, explain what we found out, and ask him to consider a Teen Challenge program[4] instead of jail time."

"Certainly, can't hurt," Kleg smiled. "I'll add that to my prayers."

Kleg and I showed up at the court hearing on Janet's behalf. No family or friends cared enough to support her. Despite a prior conviction, the judge graciously granted her leniency.

"I will give you one last chance to turn your life around, young lady," he warned. "Since these people have come on your behalf, I will allow you to go to the Teen Challenge program—but the next time you come before this court, I will not show you leniency."

Thank you, Jesus! I couldn't wait to see the girls' faces when Janet walked into the house. This would undoubtedly strengthen their faith as much as it did mine.

After celebrating Janet's victory, I drove her to the Teen Challenge program. Before she entered the program, I said, "Janet, the judge gave you this opportunity. You'd be in jail if God didn't intervene. Please give the program a chance."

"I know, Pam. You and the girls have been great. No one's ever cared enough to help me." I prayed one last prayer with her before she hugged me goodbye.

Two weeks later, I received a phone call from the program informing me Janet ran away. My heart sank. It seemed she didn't like the discipline and had a personality conflict with the supervisor. I hoped she might come back to us, but I never heard from her again. When I told the girls that Janet didn't make it in the program, they were shocked.

They wanted to know, "How could she run away after everything God did for her?"

"Healing is a process," I said, "it takes time. All we can do is our best, but, ultimately, we have to leave the results in God's hands." Disappointment showed in their faces.

"Hey, didn't God answer our prayers and cause the judge to give her a chance instead of jail time? Wasn't that a miracle?"

"That sure was," one of the girls said.

"Didn't God do his part to help Janet?" They all nodded.

"Janet just wasn't ready to do hers. I think she's still too young to understand the consequences of her choices."

"When they catch up with her, she will," Vicky said and shook her head.

"I know Janet will always remember what God did for her," I said, "He poured a little of his love into her heart through you girls and our prayers. Maybe one day she will find her way to him."

I received an urgent call from a friend whose fourteen-year-old daughter went missing. The police suspected she might have been involved with a gang at the local mall. Teenage gang recruitment was rampant.

"Pam, the police are doing all they can, but do you have any ideas that might help?" His voice was full of desperation.

"I'm not sure. Let me talk to Vicky."

Vicky said, "If you take me to the mall, I'll find out what I can." She could identify gang members and talk their language. She had a better chance of getting information than the police. We drove to the mall in the San Fernando Valley where his daughter had last been seen.

We entered the busy mall, and Vicky said, "You better stay here while I check it out." Vicky left to investigate, and I ordered a coffee and waited. She returned later with good news. "Ok, here's the deal. I talked to this guy who told me who she might be with. After the malls close, there's a club where a lot of gangs hang out."

"Really? That's great. I'll call her father."

"We don't know if she's there. Let's go see before we call her father." She was right.

I drove to the club and parked a safe distance from the entrance but close enough to see who came and went. We waited. Finally, I spotted the missing daughter going into the club with two men.

"There she is, Vicky! That's her. I'm calling her father now."

I called her father, told him we located his daughter, gave him our location, and he alerted the police. While they were on their way, we kept our eyes on the door to make sure she didn't leave.

"OK, I'm going in. I'm afraid of what that gang might do to her."

"No . . . Vicky . . . wait for the police!" She bounded out of the car and moved toward the entrance. She disappeared into the club as I prayed for her protection. Where are the police? What's taking them so long?

When the club door opened, Vicky emerged with the girl just as the police and her father arrived. He rushed to embrace his daughter, who wept in her grateful father's arms. The police arrested the gang leaders.

God had a purpose for Vicky, and he used her to save this young girl's life. She made a valuable contribution to my work in the ministry—she became a gift from God—a gift I almost rejected.

I learned how God is always working in me, even as he is working through me.

Chapter Fourteen:
Crossroads

LETTING GO AND TRUSTING GOD

He will wipe every tear from their eyes. There will be no more death or mourning or crying or pain, for the old order of things has passed away.

Revelation 21:4

"**I** have to go to New York for a few days," Ed said. "Can you stay at the house while I'm gone?"

"Sure," I answered eagerly. It wasn't too often I had a break from the ministry.

"There's a package that needs to go to the office. Would you mind dropping it off?"

"No problem!" It would be fun seeing old friends over at the Paramount studio.

Coming out of Ed's office, I bumped into Jim Brooks, creator of the *Mary Tyler Moore Show*. Ed and I spent time with him and his then-girlfriend, Holly, at social functions. "Pam, what are you doing here?"

"I dropped something off for Ed." I smiled, "How are you?"

"Come in and sit for a minute."

I planned to drop off several Christian albums to Al Cory, President of RSO Records, and then have lunch with my friend Janis, his executive assistant. I got caught up in our conversation and forgot the time.

"Oh, wow, I have to run." I said, "It was great seeing you and catching up." I gave Jim a hug and thanked him for his time and rushed off to keep my appointments.

Something was wrong . . . I paced up and down Gower Street until I saw it . . . the empty space where I parked the car. Someone stole Ed's

Mercedes! I froze in stunned disbelief. Panic overtook me, and I ran back to the office to tell his secretary. She immediately wanted to call Ed.

"No, wait. We'll get it back," I said. "I'm sure we'll find it." I hoped to recover it before Ed came back from New York.

Stan, Ed's partner, overheard our conversation and said, "Pam, you need to let Ed know right away."

"OK, Stan—I'll call him as soon as I get home." Ed's secretary drove me back to his house. The knots in my stomach tightened as I reached for the phone to call Ed. After explaining the situation, I said, "I know we'll get it back."

"Who will want it?" he said, "Whoever stole it will have it stripped down, and there won't be much left."

I went to my weekly Bible study and asked for prayer. During prayer, an image of Ed's Mercedes parked under a tree on a quiet street formed in my mind. The car didn't appear damaged, but the location was unfamiliar. Was this wishful thinking or God showing me the answer to my prayer?

The next day the police called, "We found your car. A neighborhood watch group noticed an unfamiliar car on their street and reported it."

"Is it drivable?"

"Yes, you can make arrangements to pick it up."

They found the car before I finished filing the insurance report. Amazingly, the only things taken were the Christian albums.

I called Ed at the Plaza Hotel, but he was out. I left a specific message with the operator, "Please tell Mr. Weinberger, 'Your white chariot has been released from heaven all in one piece.'"

Ed called the following morning. I couldn't contain my excitement and said, "I told you we'd get it back!"

"Yes, that's great."

I could hear the little chuckle in his voice.

To celebrate the end of our three-month School of Discipleship, the class suggested an all-night prayer meeting, but we needed a location. Ed's house would be perfect, but I doubted he'd agree to such an unusual request. I mustered my courage and asked Ed if I could use the house.

He surprised me when he said, "OK, you can use the house—just don't burn any crosses on the front lawn."

Ed booked a room at the Beverly Wilshire Hotel while we spent the night in prayer. Ed's kind generosity never ceased to amaze me. Allowing me to use the house for an all-night prayer meeting went beyond any standard request. After we put the house back in perfect order, we prayed a blessing over it and all those who lived there.

I made all the innocent mistakes young Christians do when sharing their newfound faith. In my enthusiasm, I left Christian tracts like the "Four Spiritual Laws" in the bathroom, by the telephone, and other Christian literature scattered around the house. It disappointed me when I found them relegated to the trash.

Ed and I were standing in the kitchen discussing his upcoming schedule. Without realizing the impact my statement might have, I innocently said, "Ed, do you remember when you told me you couldn't change and I argued semantics with you? Well, I have to apologize for that. You're right. Without Jesus, a person can't change."

With that, he exploded. I stood dumbfounded, bewildered. He stormed upstairs as I followed. He turned with glaring eyes and snapped, "I'm Jewish."

"I thought that was your nationality."

I didn't know he perceived his Jewish heritage in a religious light. He had an etching of Jesus with a crown of thorns labeled "Man of Sorrows" on a shelf in his house.

He crossed to the upstairs landing and demanded, "You and your God get out of my house!" And slammed the door.

I stood paralyzed. I could almost feel Jesus take my hand and say, "Let's go." His presence led me down the stairs and outside to my car.

Torrents of tears blurred my vision. I didn't have anywhere to go. I wasn't in any condition to go back to the ministry, so I ended up on the floor in the back corner of a Christian bookstore in Westwood. The Christian music soothed my punctured heart.

After wiping my tears, I read through the inspirational cards and found one that expressed my regret and wrote Ed a note of apology. Even though we had different beliefs, I wanted him to know I respected his right of choice. The next day I left it on the table in his kitchen.

He called me a few days later, "I have to work late and want to know if you can walk Angus." We never mentioned the incident or my card again.

I hadn't heard from Ed for several months, so it surprised me when he called. We chatted for a few minutes about the animals and how things were going before he said, "Jim Brooks is getting married, and I wanted to know if you'd like to go?"

"Really? That's wonderful." Jim and Holly had dated for a while. "Where are they getting married?"

"They're planning a small wedding in the garden at Jim's house in Malibu. Just a few close friends. Do you want to go?"

"I'd love to." I looked forward to catching up with Ed.

A few cast members from the *Mary Tyler Moore Show* and other friends and celebrities attended. The fresh sea breeze blew away the intensity of my daily concerns, and I drank in the peace of the Pacific Ocean. As I wandered around greeting folks and listening to the stimulating conversations, I drifted over to a small group gathered around Jim and Mary Tyler Moore. I stood next to Mary as they chatted. I reached into my purse for my handkerchief and gently wiped Mary's nose then placed it back in my purse as though nothing had happened. I thought I'd been discreet, but Mary stared at me, horrified.

"Sorry, Mary, but you had a little thingamajig on your nose," I said timidly and pressed my finger to my nose. Everyone stifled their amusement as the group dispersed.

I went back to sit with Ed. "I think Mary's upset with me," I said, but the story had already reached him. He shook his head and could barely look at me without bursting into laughter.

"What was I supposed to do?" I said, "She had something on her nose. Didn't anyone see it?"

Of course, they did, but no one dared to tell Mary. They let her walk around, oblivious to the little thingamajig on her nose.

These were the times I appreciated Ed's sense of humor. God bless the comedy writers who find humor in the most embarrassing moments.

The day came when the Lord confronted me, "What is more important, your financial security or Ed's salvation?"

"What do you mean, Lord?" I balked.

Ed's financial support helped while I worked in the ministry. It also kept us connected. Though we couldn't make the relationship work, we still cared for each other and shared our animals. I appreciated his kindness.

God seemed to be asking for a deeper commitment. As long as I relied on Ed financially, he would never understand God's faithfulness to provide for me. This financial cord needed to be severed for me to walk entirely by faith.

I understood the principle in theory but feared two things. First, I didn't want to completely let go of my friendship with Ed, and second, I didn't know if I could trust God enough to provide financially.

My faith grew gradually, and the transformation took place in the process. God didn't require me to do this when I first became a Christian.

I thought God's provision came through Ed's generosity. His support gave me time to experience God's faithfulness until I had enough trust to take this next step. Ed's salvation meant more than any financial security.

Matthew 6:24 kept running through my head: "No one can serve two masters. Either you will hate the one and love the other, or you will be devoted to the one and despise the other. You cannot serve God and Money."

I lived in a condemned house that could be torn down any day, my groceries came from the local food bank, and I shopped for clothes out of the donation bags given to the ministry. The only money I had is what Ed gave me. God must be testing my faith. Could he be asking for the last remnant of my self-sufficiency? I had to wrestle my fears to the ground. The battle ensued between my flesh and the Spirit . . . and my heart.

I took another step of faith that day and wrote Ed a letter. I expressed my gratitude for all his kindness. I asked him to forgive me for any past misunderstandings and released him from his financial support.

I prayed my letter conveyed my love for him and all our relationship meant to me. I wept as I wrote it and shed tears as I left it on the dining room table. My tears continued as I opened the front door, and there, shining radiantly, was the most glorious rainbow arched across the sky.

The rainbow symbolizes God's beautiful promise of hope, and reminded me that God understood my pain. My love for him outweighed any sacrifice he required of me. His tenderness caressed me as I closed the door behind me.

Periodically I kept in touch with Ed. I'd call him on his birthday and during the Christmas holidays. The last time I spoke to him he told me he had a son.

"A son," I said. "Are you married?"

"No."

"Are you happy?"

"Happy?" he said. "What do you mean 'happy'? What's happy?"

I didn't think I asked a profoundly philosophical question.

"Congratulations," I said. "Can I meet your son?"

"If you want to."

We arranged for my visit, and the following week I arrived at the house. Carlene, the mother of his son, opened the door and graciously welcomed me with a warm smile.

When I entered the house, it surprised me how many memories resurfaced and flooded me with emotions—in that corner I trimmed Ed's first Christmas tree—his eyes shone with boyish glee when I lit the colorful lights. We had fun that year. I ran my hand along the sofa table I once lined with candles on his birthday. I had to shake myself out of the past and force myself to focus on the present.

Carlene escorted me upstairs to the nursery, where I noticed all the improvements made to the house. She placed her newborn son in my arms, "Oh my gosh, he looks exactly like Ed." Holding Ed's beautiful baby boy made me wonder what my life would be like if we had stayed together.

"You think you know someone, and then they do something completely out of context," Carlene said. "Ed never talks about his past, but when he told me you were coming, he told me to be *nice* to you, that you had a spiritual experience."

I hoped Ed respected my choices—even if he didn't agree with them.

After congratulating Carlene on the birth of her son, I thanked her for her time and left. I drove down Sunset Plaza Drive knowing this would be for the last time. Ed had a woman who loved him, a son, and a life where I no longer belonged. The time came to completely let go. I never saw or spoke with Ed after that for almost twenty years.

It wasn't until I attended a birthday celebration at the Peninsula Hotel in Beverly Hills that we bumped into each other again. Walking down the hall, I caught the side of a man's face that reminded me of Ed.

"Mr. Weinberger?" I said. The man spun around. There stood Ed after all these years.

"Ed! How are you?" I beamed and gave him a hug.

Ever the gentleman, he invited me to sit and offered me some tea. We sat and chatted for a few minutes. Ed told me about his two boys and asked me what I did.

"I'm a marriage and family therapist."

"Are you married?"

"No, I never married."

"How can you be a marriage therapist if you're not married?"

I laughed. I didn't want to tell him how much I learned about relationships from what *didn't* work in ours, so I said, "I went to school and got my master's degree."

"Well, don't give up hope—it could still happen."

I smiled at his sweetness.

He had a meeting to go to, and I had friends waiting. We hugged goodbye, and I thanked him for the tea.

Watching him walk away left me with a strange poignancy. My heart flooded with gratitude for having loved this man and all the memories we shared. I appreciated the healing God did in my heart as the door to my past, once again, gently closed.

THE BEAUTY
OF
RESTORATION

Chapter Fifteen:
Treasures in the Wilderness

DEEPER HEALING

He found him in a desert land,
And in the wasteland, a howling wilderness;
He encircled him, He instructed him,
He kept him as the apple of His eye.

Deuteronomy 32:10 NKJV

The chaos of crisis became my new normal. Amid the turmoil, my peace came when I gave up control and surrendered my inadequacies to God. When I yielded my will, he stepped in to reveal his faithfulness.

I never understood how God could sort out the most unbelievable situations, but he always came through with some out-of-the-box answer. I began to trust that what Jesus said is true for us today: nothing is impossible[5] for God. Solutions appeared in answer to our desperate prayers: money arrived when most needed, phone calls came with opportunities, and favor turned hearts set against us. Through his inspired interventions, I experienced a different aspect of God and marveled at his creativity and sheer goodness.

My faith began to expect God's consistent acts of kindness. His faithfulness in extreme situations had an extraordinary faith-building effect. He never ran out of miracles.

That's why I didn't understand a new shift in my prayers. I couldn't get past this sense of limitation. I hit a spiritual ceiling and couldn't break through. When I asked the Lord about it, I heard a small voice inside me say, "I have more for you to learn. It's time to move."

"Really?" I tensed. "I'm not sure I can handle *more*."

I didn't look forward to telling Kleg. I bolstered myself and approached his office.

"Kleg, I think God is going to move me."

"What?" He looked up from his desk, his face registering surprise. "Where are you going?"

I shrugged my shoulders. "I have no idea."

"Then why are you leaving?" I knew it would be hard for him to understand.

"Remember when Alice from *Alice in Wonderland* bumped her head on the ceiling?" I laughed at how silly that sounded. "I feel like I'm bumping my head against a spiritual ceiling." It's the only way I could describe it.

"I'm sorry to hear that." He frowned and pushed some papers aside. "We're sure going to miss you, Pam." He lifted his eyes to mine, "You really have a heart for these women. I know wherever God is going to take you, you'll be a blessing." His disappointment saddened me. "You can stay here as long as you need."

"Thank you, Kleg. I've learned so much from you."

Two weeks later, I received a phone call from my Pastor, Kenn, "I think Brent might have an opportunity you'd be interested in." Brent Rue, one of the Vineyard pastors who taught at the School of Discipleship, had a thriving church in Lancaster about an hour outside Los Angeles. "Give him a call and let him tell you about it."

I knew Brent and his wife, Happy when they were on staff at the Vineyard in West Los Angeles. They started a Bible study in Lancaster that grew into a church plant in the Mojave Desert.

I called the next day, "Just the person I want to talk to," Brent said. "Dr. Gross from Palmdale General Hospital contacted me to see if our church wanted to use their real estate properties for house ministries."

"Who is Dr. Gross?"

"He's the clinical director of the psychiatric unit at the hospital. Kenn thought, since you ran the crisis house in Hollywood, you might be interested."

"I might be, but I'd need to know more about it."

"Let me give you Frank Marklin's number. He's Dr. Gross's partner, and you can discuss it with him." Frank and I decided to meet in Lancaster to discuss the project and show me the house.

The drive to the meeting gave me time to think. Surrounded by barren sand dotted with yucca trees and little else, I wondered, *Why the desert? Couldn't God have chosen a place near the ocean or the mountains?* I loved either of these locations—the desert not so much.

As I meditated on the Biblical significance of desert life, I remembered the honored patriarchs whose lives were changed in the desert. Moses went to the desert[6] and encountered a burning bush, Jesus was "led by the Spirit" into the desert, and Paul went to the desert before returning to Jerusalem. We all have wilderness experiences, but I never thought mine would be so literal.

After the hour drive, it felt good to stretch my legs as I walked into Denny's restaurant. Frank greeted me with a warm smile. He had a gentle demeanor and appeared to be in his early 40s. We ordered coffee.

"Dr. Gross and I are getting involved in real estate and thought the church could use the houses. Brent told me you're the director of a crisis house in Hollywood."

"Yes, but this would be a big move for me." I knew nothing about Frank or the hospital and asked, "What do you and Dr. Gross do at the hospital?"

"Dr. Gross is the clinical psychologist, and I run the process groups on the psychiatric unit. We're pioneering a specialized Christian therapy program inside our traditional unit." That thought intrigued me.

"Right now, we have one house we're planning to convert into an executive recovery home for professionals struggling with alcoholism, but until we complete the plans, we thought the church could use it."

We drove over to the house for a walk through. It needed work, but with five bedrooms and two living rooms, it had potential. I thanked Frank for his time, told him I would get back to him after I prayed about it, and then headed home.

My tension eased as I entered the driveway and saw the girls wave from the back porch. Breezing past Kleg with a quick nod, I disappeared up the stairs to my room. The thought of leaving Hollywood made me apprehensive. As difficult as the move into the crisis house had been, I still had access to my friends, my church, city life, and familiar resources. The thought of being cut off from everything and everyone unsettled me.

Could this be the move God impressed on me? I knew Brent and Happy, and I'd still be part of the Vineyard churches. If it didn't work, I could always come back. It seemed God opened this door, but I still had to choose if I wanted to make the move to Lancaster.

I didn't know what Vicky would do if I left. For her to continue growing in her faith, she needed to get away from the Hollywood influence lurking right outside our doors. I didn't want the streets to tempt her back again. She proved herself trustworthy, and I valued her friendship.

After praying about it, I decided to take another step of faith and move to the desert, but I wanted Vicky to come with me.

Kleg's knit brow told me he had concerns, "I'm not sure that's such a good idea."

"Why not?" I knew what I thought he'd say.

"I think she'll become too dependent on you."

"I know, but we have sent her to programs that never worked, and she can't stay here. I can't put her back on the street, and besides, she deserves this opportunity." I paused. "I'll also need someone to help me."

When I told Vicky, she was thrilled. We packed our bags and headed up the highway to the next adventure that lay ahead.

Once we moved into the house, the church began to send homeless Christians, and the hospital sent a couple of outpatients from their psychiatric program. We lived on donations from the church, eggs from the hatchery, food bank supplies, and the grace of God. I became a creative chef with egg dishes and potatoes.

My favorite amethyst ring stayed in a small dish on the counter in my bathroom. Ed gave it to me one Christmas, and it carried sentimental value. When I reached for it one morning, the dish was empty. After a thorough search, I realized someone must have taken the ring. I became furious. I ran downstairs and called everyone together.

"No one is leaving this house until my ring is returned. I don't care who took it. I want it back." I told Vicky to make sure no one left.

"I am going out, and when I get back, I want my ring returned." I needed to leave the house and get a handle on my emotions.

I dashed to the desert in the back of our house. My anger turned into tears of rage as I picked up a dead branch from a yucca tree and slammed it against another tree. It cracked in two from the force of the impact. I continued to pick up branch after branch and either slammed them into trees or pounded them into the desert sand. I cried to God, "This is what I get for my obedience? You let them steal my ring!"

The desert allowed me the privacy of my pain. It wasn't the loss of the ring, as much as my disappointment in God for allowing it to happen. I continued to fume until I slumped in a heap on the desert floor.

The gentle voice I came to know as the Lord whispered, "Are you ready to listen?"

I trembled like a child about to be scolded by her father. But God didn't chastise me for being petulant. "I understand your pain, but there are deeper things I want to heal in your heart." His words soothed my raw emotions.

It's in those moments where "the goodness of the LORD[7] leads to repentance." God's tender voice comforted me, but I wondered about the "deeper things." His merciful love drew me closer, and I turned the situation over to him. My anger dissolved, and I returned to the house.

I darted upstairs to my bedroom to wash my face. As I walked across the ugly, shag carpet, I stepped on an object that felt like a stone. I reached down to remove it only to find it was my ring. I sank onto the edge of my bed and stared at it. Someone must have tossed it into my room. I went downstairs and thanked the girls before apologizing for my attitude.

God used my ring to shed light on my attachment to my former life. Thinking I had surrendered *all* to Jesus, this revelation came as a shock. Surrender is a process. It's not a once-and-done. It's a day-by-day choice. God is the only one who can reveal those hidden areas in our hearts.

> The heart is deceitful above all things,
> And desperately wicked;
> Who can know it?
> I, the LORD, search the heart.
> (Jeremiah 17:9–10 NKJV)

Learning to trust an invisible God is one of heaven's great mysteries. Trust takes time to develop. I learn to trust my friends through shared experiences that, over time, will prove them dependable—or not. Every human being will ultimately fail me. They have to because they are not perfect and are still in process themselves. God is the only one who will never fail me. I may not always like his ways because they are higher than my ways, but if I hold on to my faith when I don't understand, he will show me the truth of his purposes in his time. These times became the real test of my faith. These are the times God tests me and my commitment to him. Do I love him for who he is or for what he does for me? Once I know I can trust God, it's easier for me to extend grace when others disappoint me.

As I engage with God, I learn to understand his true nature. When I risk being authentic, I experience his understanding. God encourages us in Isaiah 1:18 to come and reason with him. When I realize how reasonable God is, I *want* to listen for his wisdom. His unconditional love removes the fear of punishment so I can learn what he wants to teach me. I learn to welcome correction and the removal of impediments to my growth, blocking my freedom. Knowing he loves me, even in my imperfection, strengthens my trust in him.

The more I learn to trust his passion for me, the more I fall in love with him. His love is strong enough to heal any pain in my heart and reveals the wisdom of his ways. At the time, I didn't understand the process, but in retrospect, as Psalm 136 and 1 Corinthians 13 promise, *his love endures forever, and his love never fails me.*

After several months the doctors abandoned their initial idea of a recovery facility and put the house up for sale. "Don't worry, Pam, we're buying several smaller houses," Frank said. "I'll take you over to the one we think you'll like."

On the ride over to the new house, I asked Frank, "Do you think mixing mental health patients with struggling Christians is a good idea?"

"Why? What are you concerned about?"

"I've noticed that the women from the hospital are more fragile. There needs are more complex than the other girls. So, I have to deal with them differently."

"That's true. They don't have the same resources to draw from and are more complicated."

"I think we should make this new home exclusively a mental health rehabilitation home for outpatients from the hospital."

"Interesting. That could work. Let's talk to Dr. Gross and Brent and see what they think."

After several discussions, we agreed to make my house a recovery home for outpatients from the hospital, and the church would use the other houses for church ministry. The doctors bought a more functional home for me. This time, I had a home that wasn't waiting to be torn down or used for another purpose. This home was just for us.

Our new modest home, formerly a foster home, adequately met our needs. The four bedrooms accommodated two girls each. We joined two picnic tables in the center of the large kitchen for dining, art classes, and other group activities. It had a fenced-in backyard, and the garage had been converted into a bedroom suite with an office and bathroom, which gave me the privacy I needed.

It wasn't long before the reality of my commitment hit me with a devastating impact. What was I doing on the backside of the desert living with eight women from the psychiatric unit? What did I know about mental health? What kind of care would these women need? I felt totally in over my head, ill-equipped, and definitely unqualified.

I had only spent a little over a year running a women's crisis house in Hollywood and attended a three-month school of discipleship program. I was less than two years into my spiritual journey. God always seemed to throw me into the deep end of the pool, where I had to hold onto him as he taught me how to swim.

The day-to-day needs kept me busy until I fell into bed. Exhausted, I had no problem falling asleep, but a few hours later, I woke up gasping for air, with my heart pounding. My skin crawled with a tingling sensation as I felt like I disintegrated into a million particles and vanished into the darkness.

I'd never experienced such a surreal experience before. I prayed and paced the length of my room. My breathing eased, and I climbed back into bed praying in my prayer language. This happened for two more consecutive nights. I had no idea why this happened and started to wonder, *Did I make a mistake coming to the desert? What am I doing here?* The thoughts tormented me, and I had no control over the anxiety.

"God, I can't handle this responsibility." I began to weep.

"Wait!" I shook myself. "This isn't my responsibility. It's yours." Suddenly I understood. "This is your ministry—not mine. These are your women—not mine."

I didn't recognize how much self-sufficiency had unknowingly crept into my thinking. I started to believe that I'm the one doing God's work instead of God doing it through me. My pride wanted to believe itself capable of doing what only God could do. Once I reminded myself of that truth, my peace returned.

If I made a mistake, God knew I did it with a pure heart. I took a step of faith based on what I thought he said. I didn't believe God would condemn me if I didn't get it right. If I misunderstood, I knew he would redirect me to the right path.

Abraham must have felt the same way when he left his home and family in Ur of the Chaldeans to follow God. As the writer of Hebrews later informed us, Abraham didn't have a clue[8] where God would lead him, but by faith, he went. After I submitted these women's needs into God's hands, I never had another panic attack again.

I settled into my new home and began creating a healing environment to teach these women skills to help them function better in society. Even though they carried psychological labels, such as schizoaffective disorder or bipolar disorder, I treated them with respect like normal human beings, not invalids. They continued to take their medications and see their psychiatrist, but I trusted God to do the healing through love, understanding, and the application of his Word.

We had daily schedules of activities, house meetings, Bible studies, and Sunday church services. They all participated in household chores, took turns cooking, and learned to keep their rooms clean and practice daily hygiene. They became part of the day-to-day running of the house. I wanted to foster their independence so they could maintain a life outside of institutions. Once they learned how to take responsibility for their choices, their confidence strengthened.

Vicky began to thrive in the desert. Away from the tension of the Hollywood streets, her charismatic personality began to emerge, and she started making friends at the church.

I received a surprise phone call from my pastor, Kenn, "Pam, I don't know if you know this, but Joanie's dad is a dentist." Joanie, Kenn's beautiful wife, is greatly respected for her gentle and loving spirit. Not many are as generous as she and her husband.

"No, I didn't know that."

"Joanie told her dad about Vicky, and he agreed to fix her teeth for free."

"Wow! That is awesome!" I couldn't wait to tell Vicky.

"Joanie will make the arrangements and give you a call."

"Thank you, Kenn. I know Vicky will be thrilled."

"Give her our love, and tell her she's in our prayers."

When I told Vicky about Kenn's phone call, her eyes moistened with gratitude, "Are you kidding me?" Her smile radiated her unbridled joy, and she jumped up and down like a little kid. "What a miracle!"

Vicky continued to blossom and inspired my faith. Now, with her new teeth, long flowing black hair, and cute dimples, she began to embrace her femininity. Her transformation continued to evolve, and Vicky became a different person from the one I met two years earlier. She was hired to work for a county program as a counselor helping recovering alcoholics.

The Desert Vineyard embraced my merry band of misfits as a part of their community and made them welcome. Their love and support helped us all learn and grow together.

Frank and Vicky with a cup she painted for him

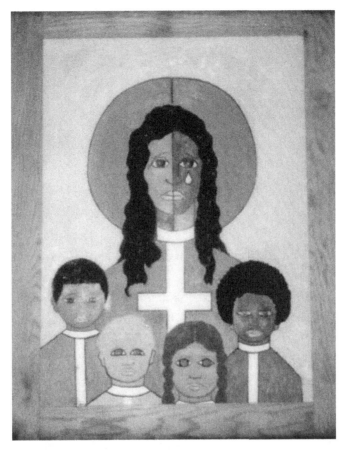

Vicky's original oil painting: Jesus and the Little Children

Chapter Sixteen:
Mentors and Mercy

CHRISTIAN THERAPY

*Now to Him who is able to do exceedingly abundantly above all
that we ask or think, according to the power that works in us.*

Ephesians 3:20 NKJV

As I stood at the nurse's station on the psychiatric unit, a giant man wearing cowboy boots and a doctor's lab coat moseyed down the hall toward us.

"Who is that man?" I asked the nurse.

"That's Dr. Nichols," she said, "He's the one God told to build this hospital."

"Really?"

"You'll love him," she smiled. "I've never met a doctor like him." Her face lit up with respect for him. "He saved my cousin's life. All the other doctors said she wouldn't make it, but Dr. Nichols sat by her bed and prayed for her." She leaned towards me and whispered, "I saw the tears in his eyes."

"That's my kind of doctor. Too bad there are not more like him."

"Wait until you meet his wife, June. She is the queen of compassion."

Dr. Nichols stopped to give a bear hug to an attendant.

"Does he always do that?"

"Yes," the nurse chuckled, "no one gets away from his hugs."

She moved from behind the station to greet the doctor. He lifted her tiny frame off the floor. "How are you and your cousin doing?"

"Fine, Dr. Nichols," she giggled. "This is Pam. She runs the house for our outpatients."

Before I knew it, he wrapped me in a warm embrace.

"God bless you," he said. "We've needed a home like that."

"Have you seen my wife?" he asked Doris, the head nurse.

"I think she's in with Dr. Gross."

He turned to me, "Have you met my wife?"

"Not yet."

"Come with me." He grabbed my hand and led me down the hall.

The sun poured in through the window that overlooked the patients' patio as we entered Dr. Gross's office. "Look who I found. This is Pam. She works with our outpatients."

Mrs. Nichols rose to hug me. "Welcome." She equaled her husband in stature.

"Glad to meet you, Pam. Frank has told me all about you." Dr. Gross said as he greeted me from behind his desk.

What am I doing in a psychiatric hospital? *This* must be the *more* God told me about. These professional Christians were dedicated to healing, and their acceptance eased my concern.

When I became an adult, my mother told me about her sister Florence, whom we visited once when I attended middle school. All I remember is how strange my aunt seemed sitting hunched over on a bench clutching her purse. "When Florence became pregnant out of wedlock, your grandmother forced her to marry the baby's father." She paused. "He abused her for years, and when she tried to commit suicide, he committed her to an asylum." She took a deep breath and swallowed. "By the time she could be released she had been institutionalized. She spent too many years as a patient in the hospital." Tears formed in my mother's eyes, "none of us knew how to care for her, and she passed away in the hospital."

"How come I never knew?"

"We were ashamed and didn't know what to do, so we never talked about her."

The 1948 movie *Snake Pit* depicted the horrors of mental illness and the institutions. Ken Kesey's 1962 novel, *One Flew Over the Cuckoo's Nest,* became a film in 1975 starring Jack Nicholson and won five Academy Awards. It horrified me when they gave him a lobotomy.

Dr. Nichols encountered many attacks from the medical and psychiatric communities when he supported the Christian Therapy Program. This approach to psycho-socio-spiritual healing in an integrated manner based on the Word of God clashed with traditional psychiatry, which considered hearing voices, including God's voice, delusional at the time. The Christian Therapy Program had to establish psychological credibility for Biblical principles and demonstrate how they benefited mental health treatment.

The Christian therapy program was a specialized track within the traditional psychiatric program. The patients who requested Christian therapy were asked to sign a special waiver to be part of the groups. The patients who participated shared their experiences with the other patients on the unit: who, when they heard about their breakthroughs, often decided to sign up themselves. The staff never proselytized the patients and remained professional.

At the same time, the Christian community didn't believe any psychological approach had relevance to Biblical healing. There needed to be a comprehensive Biblical foundation for these interventions. The doctors fought battles on both fronts.

My work at the hospital exposed me to another aspect of God's kingdom. These professionals went about the business of loving those who were seen as unlovable. Their approach to patient care inspired me.

When I entered the psychiatric unit for the first time and heard the giant doors lock behind me, I had to force myself to breathe. My claustrophobia dissipated once I reached the nurses' station. Over time I outgrew my fears of being trapped on a unit with unstable patients.

"Frank is starting a group," Doris, the head nurse, said. "Let's sit in."

We slipped into the large group room. The windows let in enough light to brighten the room. The patients sat in a circle, and Frank started a simple warm-up exercise to engage the group. After they relaxed, Frank said, "Who wants to work today?" Several patients raised their hands, but Frank chose an older, quiet woman who needed a breakthrough before being discharged.

"How about we work on your mother?" He took her hand and led her to the center of the circle. He sat her in one of the two chairs facing each other.

"I'm fine." She hesitated. "I forgave her long ago." Frank asked her to choose a patient who most resembled her mother. She chose one of the more demanding patients to role-play her mother, and the stand-in sat in one chair while Frank sat his hesitant patient in the opposite chair.

"Ok, I want you to start talking to her as if she were your mother. Tell her what you forgave her for."

"I can't . . . I can't do it Frank," she stuttered.

"Sure, you can. Go ahead. Tell your mother what it was like as a child." The patient started to shake and cried, "You were never there for me. I was scared at night."

"Stop being so weak," the woman role-playing her mother said. "You were always so clingy."

This triggered the patient, and she shouted, "Stop calling me weak! I'm not weak." Frank encouraged her to keep going.

"Nothing I ever did was good enough. I could never please you. All you thought about was yourself!"

Frank handed her a Kleenex.

"I couldn't wait to get away from you, so I married the first man who showed me any affection."

Frank handed her a Bataka[9], a stick with a cloth foam cover used for anger management, and placed an empty metal chair in front of her. "Go ahead and hit the chair." She banged the chair with a force that surprised her.

"I needed a mother!" She hit the chair again before she threw the Bataka on the floor and crumpled in tears.

I sat riveted as the process unfolded.

Frank put his hand on her back and said, "Can you forgive her now?"

"I want to—I had no idea I still had so much anger. Yes, I forgive you, Mom."

Frank hugged her, and the group applauded her honest work. Frank hugged the patient who did the role-play and made sure she was okay.

"How did you like the group?" Frank said as we exited the group room.

"I had no idea how much pain these patients carry."

Frank's expertise helped expose their unresolved emotions.

"You can't heal what you can't feel," he said. "Let me take you to lunch."

As we sat in the hospital cafeteria, I asked Frank, "As new creations in Christ, aren't we supposed to put the past behind us?" I didn't understand. "Why focus on the past?"

Frank cut his sandwich in half. "How can you put the past behind you if you still carry the emotions inside?"

"Do we have to release those repressed emotions before there's healing?" I asked, trying to get to the root of the approach. "But that patient said she forgave her mother, so why did you put her in the chair?"

"When she had to confront her mother, she discovered how much anger she still had buried inside." He sipped his iced tea.

"When she started yelling, it really surprised me." I laughed. "Who would have thought that quiet little woman had so much anger."

"That's my point. That quiet little woman forgave her mother out of principle, but not out of her emotional pain." He finished his sandwich. "If you don't clear the emotional trauma, it builds defenses that can emotionally block you."

"Is that why people become alcoholics or addicts? Because they're trying to block old pain?"

"That's how they numb their emotions, but they also have a network of negative beliefs causing them guilt and shame."

We picked up our trays, emptied them, and headed back to the unit.

"So, what you're saying is that if we don't deal with the painful things from our past, those old emotions can cause us to react in defensive and destructive ways?"

Frank smiled and answered my question with a question. "How can you *manage* what you can't identify or understand? Then your feelings are in control."

"You make it sound so simple." He had a gift of cutting to the bottom line.

Dr. Gross and Frank ran groups covering grief/loss, anger management and trauma/abuse issues, all with phenomenal results. The spontaneous scenarios of the real-life pain in a patient's life outweighed any improvisational workshop I attended in Hollywood.

Dr. Gross and Frank used role-play and the Gestalt technique, developed by Fritz Perls in the 1940s, as an alternative to conventional psychoanalysis. The empty chair technique was effective in confronting and helping resolve past conflicts.

As I sat enthralled with the group process, Dr. Gross asked me to role-play with an older male patient, a former pastor, who had molested his daughter. The patient built a wall of denial that made repentance impossible, and he struggled with suicidal thoughts. Repentance required acknowledging what he did, how it affected his daughter, and genuine remorse—a cross too heavy for him to bear.

Dr. Gross set up two chairs facing each other.

He asked me to sit in one and the patient to sit in the other. My adrenaline spiked as I moved to the chair. I rubbed my clammy hands on my pants legs before I sat and faced the man. Dr. Gross asked me, role-playing his daughter, to express what I thought she might feel. He then moved behind the patient to help him with words when necessary.

Drawing from my acting background, I improvised. "How could you do this, Daddy?" I wanted to scream. "I thought you loved me."

"I do love you," he said. "I wanted to be closer, so you knew how much I loved you."

141

"No!" My scream burst forth. "You're supposed to protect me, not touch me like that. How can I trust any man when I can't trust my own father?"

"But I love you," he insisted. "You can trust me. I want to take care of you."

I put my hands over my ears and shouted, "Liar! You're a liar!" The group gasped. "You violated me! You molested me! That is not love!"

Dr. Gross put his hand on the patient's shoulder and whispered, "Do you see the pain she is in?" The patient squirmed and looked like he wanted to bolt. He couldn't look at me.

"I trusted you," I said on the verge of tears. "You taught me about Jesus. I can't trust him now either." The patient reached out to touch my hand, and I jumped out of my seat and shouted, "Don't you dare touch me! Don't you ever touch me again!"

He hung his head and murmured, "I am sorry."

"Louder," Dr. Gross said.

"I'm sorry," he choked out.

"Look at her." Dr. Gross insisted, "Look her in the eyes and tell her how sorry you are and ask her to forgive you."

"I can't be forgiven," he shook his head. "I don't deserve to be forgiven. God can't forgive me for what I've done."

Frank came up behind me and instructed me to bend down and take the patient's hand, "I want to forgive you, Daddy. God can forgive you, and he still loves you." This broken man flung himself toward me and wept on my shoulder. I couldn't help but cry along with the rest of the group.

Frank came over and lifted him from my shoulder, setting him back in his chair and motioning for everyone in the group to gather around. We laid hands on him and prayed for God to complete the work of healing he began. When Frank finished praying, he pulled the man from the chair and gave him a hug, followed by everyone in the group.

"Are you okay, Pam?" Dr. Gross said.

I must have looked dazed. I was. I nodded my head. "I think so."

"Good work."

I left the group room emotionally drained but spiritually exhilarated. I witnessed how the power of truth could break through the walls of denial and start the healing process, as Jesus has declared, "then you will know[10] the truth, and the truth will set you free."

"We're going to pray with a patient tomorrow," June said, "How would you like to join us?" June had a vast knowledge of the Word, and I always gained new insights from her. Vi, the lead counselor, and Doris, the head nurse, were gifted old-school Pentecostal intercessors. When a patient seemed unable to move forward in their treatment, June arranged for a special session of intercessory prayer.

The next day we gathered in the patient's room. June anointed us with oil before prayer. Then, she anointed the patient and said, "I know your heartbreak is too deep for you to bear alone, so we'd like to ask the Lord to help us bear some of that pain with you." The patient's eyes began to tear. "Is it okay if we pray in our prayer language?" The patient nodded. "You don't have to do anything except receive."

June began to pray, and the Spirit of intercession moved on our hearts. We felt the deep pain in this man's heart, and we wept alongside him. I felt like the littlest angel, dodging the wings of these mighty warrior angels taking flight in prayer.

This powerful act of intercession revealed a deeper dimension in the Spirit. We entered this spiritual realm with the power and authority of the name of Jesus and broke bondages, cleansed the deep wounds with our tears, and bore the patient's burden. God stepped into our midst and guided us with visions and words of knowledge[11]. This went past mere head knowledge and opened a spiritual portal. Our intercession tore away emotional blockages.

"God wants to heal this tragic wound in your heart." June touched his shoulder and asked, "Do you think you're ready to forgive the person who murdered your brother?"

Fresh tears filled the patient's eyes, "Yes, I want to."

God showed up in power. He heals the brokenhearted and sets the captive free. "Where two or more gather[12] in my name, there I am with them."

"Why is it so important to forgive?" asked a patient during June's Bible study on forgiveness.

"Forgiveness is the key to the kingdom," June said. "Jesus forgave those who crucified him before he entered into his Father's presence."

"I could never do that," the patient said, "They didn't deserve to be forgiven."

"Did you ask Jesus to forgive you when you were saved?"

"Yes."

"Did God show you mercy and forgive you?" June continued.

"I hope so," the patient responded.

"If God showed you mercy, don't you think he wants you to show mercy to others?"

"But I didn't murder anyone."

The group laughed.

"It doesn't matter what the crime or offense is—unforgiveness gives Satan a legal right to torment us. Don't you think that anxiety[13], depression, addiction, and fear are all tormentors?"

June read the Matthew 18 parable Jesus had related demonstrating the need to forgive others, "'The king said to him[14], "You scoundrel! Is this the way you respond to my mercy? Because you begged me, I forgave you the massive debt that you owed me. Why didn't you show the same mercy to your fellow servant that I showed to you?" In a fury of anger, the king turned him over to the prison guards to be tortured until all his debt was repaid.'"

June paused, then continued, "'In this same way[15], my heavenly Father will deal with any of you if you do not release forgiveness from your heart toward your fellow believer.'"

A patient jumped in, "Someone told me that unforgiveness is like drinking poison and expecting the other person to die." The group chuckled.

"There's no way I can forgive the person who molested me," a female patient said.

"It's hard to forgive when you have a root of bitterness, but God will give you the grace if you ask him," June said.

"I couldn't forgive my father," another patient confided, "until I used one of those Batakas in a group last week. I had so much hate, I wanted to kill him."

"That's right, forgiveness means forgiving from our heart, which is the seat of our emotions," June said. "We have to break up those strongholds and confront the anger and pain and, yes, sometimes even the murder before we can choose to forgive.

"Forgiveness doesn't mean what they did is right." She went on to explain, "It means I'm going to 'let go' of the torment it causes me and unlock the door of the prison it's kept *me* in. Forgiveness is not about the other person—it's about you and your freedom."

The process of integrating Biblical principles and therapeutic techniques made sense. Forgiveness was not just, "Oh, yeah, I forgive you, but I never want to see you again." Of course, in certain situations it may be best to set boundaries, but the emotions attached to the wounds still need cleansing from the putrefying infection caused by the injury. It means putting down the pretense, getting real, and confronting the emotions buried inside. This is not about religious condemnation but the truth that heals.

"Here's your assignment for tomorrow," June said. "I want you to write a list of all the people you can think of who have hurt and disappointed you . . . not just those who devastated or destroyed you."

"Everyone in my life will be on that list," a patient moaned.

"Yes," June laughed, "even the most well-intended people will disappoint us, but we need to forgive them if we want to stay connected to God. It's an ongoing process."

The Biblical principle of forgiveness coupled with the therapeutic intervention of role-play flushed out deep-seated emotions and brought a depth of forgiveness that cleansed the wound and liberated the patient. "Blessed be the God and Father of our Lord Jesus Christ, the Father of mercies and God of all comfort, who comforts us in all our affliction, so that we will be able to comfort those who are in any affliction, with the comfort with which we ourselves are comforted by God" (2 Corinthians 1:3–4 ESV).

I applied everything I learned at the hospital to my own life and healed right along with the patients. In addition, the freedom I experienced gave me greater insight to share with others.

People came to the hospital from all over the world and from every walk of life. Many Christian celebrities and highly visible pastors and evangelists sought the confidentiality and professional expertise of our staff. *The 700 Club*, a Christian television news magazine program, came to the hospital and interviewed Dr. Gross and the team about the program. God continued to open opportunities for more television and radio interviews. We were excited to share the healing effects of how the Biblical principles in scripture empowered the therapeutic interventions producing miraculous results.

We developed workshops on personal growth, marriage, and pastoral leadership. These workshops happened regularly at PTL's Heritage USA. Jim and Tammy Baker, the most popular international televangelist, developed a television studio and Christian retreat center and became one of the largest evangelical organizations in South Carolina.

Who thought anything this good could come from the backside of the desert? "For waters break forth in the wilderness, and streams in the desert" (Isaiah 35:6 ESV).

God birthed a new move of his Spirit, and it spilled over beyond our hospital. The Christian Therapy Hospital Program started with a specialized track in an obscure hospital and now has evolved into an internationally recognized approach to healing that has been integrated into the Christian community. As the prophet Zechariah reminds us, "Do not despise[16] small beginnings."

My father   Me   Mrs. June Nichols   Dr. Nichols

Chapter Seventeen:
Grace Builders

REWARD OF PATIENCE

As iron sharpens iron,
so one person sharpens another.

Proverbs 27:17

"I'm here to see Vi," I informed the receptionist. Vi, the lead counselor on the Christian Therapy Program, had a gift that revealed the wisdom of heaven. I admired her integrity and commitment to God.

I entered her office. "Hi Pam, this is Terri," Vi said, as she introduced the young, Jewish woman who stood wide-eyed in front of her desk, prancing in place.

"Do you have room for a new girl?" Vi continued.

I'd seen this behavior in patients on Thorazine, a medication used for psychotic conditions. They called it the "Thorazine shuffle," a side effect of the drug also known as Tardive Dyskinesia.

"Umm . . . can I talk to you, Vi?" The severity of her condition concerned me.

"Terri, can you give us a minute?" she said, "Why don't you go ask Doris how her grandkids are doing?" Terri nodded and left the office.

"You want me to take her home?"

"That would be nice," Vi smiled, "That way, Terri can be a part of the outpatient program."

"I honestly don't know if I can manage the severity of her diagnosis," I said. "Her condition is too extreme. What if she has a psychotic break and does something destructive to herself?"

"She's making progress, and I'd like that to continue."

"I know, but . . ."

"Her mother died when she was eight, and she attempted suicide at fourteen. So she's been in and out of hospitals most of her life."

"How long is she going to be on this medication? Is she still having delusions?"

"No, she's stabilizing, and I think her meds will be decreased before she's released."

I took a deep breath and sighed, "Ok, let's see how it goes."

"Thank you." Vi flashed a smile and went to get Terri.

Meanwhile, I shot up a quick prayer, "Lord help me."

They came back, and Vi said, "Terri, do you have something for Pam?"

Now what? I thought.

Terri reached down and pulled off one of her dancing shoes and dislodged a crumpled piece of paper. She handed it to me, and I carefully unfolded it. It was her disability check.

"Will that help?"

"Yes, Terri, it will. Thank you." My heart went out to this broken girl.

The primary admitting diagnosis for hospitalization in the early 80s was schizophrenia. President Reagan had signed the law preventing long-term hospitalization through the Federal Deinstitutionalization of Mentally Ill Patients called the Lanterman-Petris-Short Act[17] in 1967. With no long-term hospitalization available and the Lyons 1984 ruling that changed the definition of insanity, many of those patients were released with inadequate housing to meet their needs. Unfortunately, many became homeless and ended up on the streets and in shelters. Today, major depression is the principal admitting diagnosis for hospitalization.

I introduced Terri to the girls and settled her into her room. The doctors adjusted her medication, and the prancing stopped. The girls tried to make her comfortable and helped her get adjusted to the daily routine. Everyone participated in daily chores, aside from keeping their rooms clean, and I gave Terri the simple task of dusting.

She seemed to be blending in until Vicky confronted me. "How many times do I have to remind her to dust?" Her clipped tone revealed her frustration. "It's the easiest chore."

"She never does her chores," Cheryl piped up. "We have to remind her a thousand times."

"I'm sure it's not a thousand times, but I'll talk to her." I had sensed a growing frustration in the house, and now it became clear. Her passive-aggressive behavior upset the girls. I had my own issues with Terri but thought she needed more time to assimilate. I tried to be patient. Unfortunately, the girls didn't have the necessary tolerance needed for Terri. They were sensitive to even the slightest changes in the atmosphere.

Terri shadowed me everywhere I went, always asking questions. I knew she wanted attention, but I couldn't always give her the time she needed with eight girls and a house to run. When the questions became repetitive, my patience wore thin.

"What's for dinner?"

"Hamburgers."

"What are we having?"

"I told you, Vicky's grilling hamburgers."

"Hamburgers?"

"Yes." I continued preparing the salad for dinner.

"Why hamburgers?"

"Because that's what's on the menu."

"Can we have chicken tomorrow?"

"No, tuna casserole is on the menu." I planned the meals in advance.

"When can we have chicken?"

"Maybe next week."

"Why can't we have chicken?" she continued, unwilling to let go of her focus.

"I'll put it on the menu for next week." A part of me felt sorry for her while another part grew weary of being questioned.

"Can I go to a nutritionist?"

"A nutritionist?" *Where did this idea come from?*

"Please, I'll pay for it."

"I'll think about it." Her questions were driving me nuts.

The next day she started again, "Did you think about it? Can I go?"

"Okay, you can go." I gave up.

The following week I asked, "Did you make your appointment with the nutritionist?"

"No."

I wanted to pull my hair out. Terri affected everyone with her constant need for attention and not following through on her chores. The tensions rose.

"Where's Terri?" Loretta asked as we sat waiting to pray over dinner.

"Here I am," Terri responded as she rushed to the table. "I couldn't find my sweater."

"You always have an excuse," Vicky muttered.

And so it went, until one Sunday, we sat in the car ready to leave for church.

"Why do we always have to wait for her when we go anywhere?" Cheryl complained.

"She's always late," another girl said. Once one complained, the others chimed in. Their frustrations were understandable. The hot sun beat down on the car, making everyone more irritable. I looked at my watch and knew if she didn't come soon, we'd be late. I had to correct this before a mutiny broke out.

A few days later, I received good news. "My missionary friends have returned from India," I announced. "They're coming for dinner and a Bible study."

My friends had a ranch in the desert and worked in Third World countries. We were eager to hear about their adventures and the miracles they experienced. The girls rushed around preparing for their arrival.

After dinner and the Bible study, they prayed for all the girls.

Before leaving, my friends pulled me aside, "God has put Terri on our hearts, and we wanted to know if she could spend some time with us at the ranch."

How did they know Terri had exhausted the patience of everyone in the house? That she was dangerously close to being asked to leave? They didn't, but God did. I trusted them and said, "If Terri wants to go, it's fine with me." Terri agreed, and relief settled on the house.

We kept Terri in our prayers and asked God to bring healing into her life. When she returned a couple of weeks later, she had a light in her eyes. She smiled more and joined the girls in doing her chores.

"What happened to Terri?" Cheryl said, "She's doing better."

I didn't know if the change was permanent. Only time would tell— and it did. Terri became a joy to be around. She became a walking reflection of God's answer to prayer. God never ceases to amaze me with his perfect timing. It warmed my heart to watch Terri begin to interact positively with the girls.

Terri attached herself to Vicky and became her new best friend. They became my assistants and helped keep the house running smoothly. One day when I had a busy day of errands to run and asked if they wanted to come with me, they jumped at the chance.

"I have to make a quick stop at the bank." Next to the bank was their favorite health food store.

Terri and Vicky entreated me, "Can we go to the health food store?"

"No. I am sorry—we don't have time," I said. "I'll only be there a minute, so don't get out of the car."

After banking, I came out to an empty car. Terri and Vicky were nowhere in sight. I got into my little Volkswagen and drove out of the parking lot without them. As I headed toward the street, I looked in my rear-view mirror and saw them running out of the health food store, waving their hands shouting at me to stop. I continued on my way and ran my errands.

About an hour later, before heading home, I stopped by the parking lot to see what happened to them. They were right where I left them, two dejected rag dolls sitting on the curb—waiting. I opened the car door, "What did I say?"

"Don't get out of the car," they responded grimly.

"What did you do?"

"We got out of the car."

"Ok, just making sure you heard me."

My heart went out to the two miserable girls in my back seat. I had to bite my lip to keep from laughing.

That incident went through the house like wildfire. The next time I said, "Alright, the car's leaving for church in five minutes," the girls piled in, and Terri came running out with wet hair—barefooted and shoes and socks in hand. Everyone laughed, including Terri, who had learned her lesson.

There have to be consequences for certain behaviors. It took one time of enforcing a consequence to learn the importance of time management. It's incredible how punctuality improved.

Terri went on to finish her education, become a teacher, and purchased her first house. She lived an active life within her church community.

Terri and Pam

I never understood why God had me, in the prime of my life, living in a house full of women on the backside of the desert. Shouldn't I be socializing and looking for an eligible young man? Unfortunately, the prospects of that happening in the desert were slim to nonexistent. But when I questioned the Lord about it, I felt he had a plan for my personal life, and I didn't have to worry.

The thought God might have someone in mind allowed me to put that concern aside and focus on the work in front of me. I sensed God telling me, "You will look back on this time as a special blessing in your life." I wanted to laugh.

"Oh, really? Have you seen my schedule?" I didn't comprehend the meaning of his words, but now, as I look back, I am profoundly grateful. Between the house, the hospital, and the Vineyard, I grew in ways I never could have imagined. God's wisdom provided the answers I longed for.

I found beauty in my wilderness experience as I embraced the process of healing. The Lord purged my heart in the purifying fires of affliction. It took time, but I choose to trust instead of taking up arms against the process. New strength took root as I discovered I could survive the pain I tried to avoid. I found that "weeping lasts for a night but joy comes in the morning[18]."

The freedom on the other side of the cleansing tears taught me the pain I experienced didn't come from God. Instead, it came from the broken parts of my flesh struggling to protect itself. Too often, I believed lies. Sometimes the lies were so embedded, they felt like the truth, and the truth of God's Word felt like a lie. Before I could embrace the fullness of God's love, those lies had to be exposed and removed.

It always comes back to his will versus mine. His ways are not my ways, and when they conflict with mine, I have learned to surrender, even when I don't understand. Letting go of old negative beliefs feels like ripping adhesive tape off my soul, but joy comes when the freedom of truth is embraced.

God used the pressures of ministry to show me his faithfulness as I chose to believe his Word. He taught me the beauty of humility and the authenticity it brings. Each lie was like a broken shard being pulled from my heart, giving me the courage to continue pressing forward.

A refreshing breeze brought relief from the sweat of the day. I suggested a walk after dinner. Several of the girls came with me while Vicky and some others stayed behind to clear the table. Twilight in the desert is magical: the pink and lavender painted sky formed a background to the silhouettes of the yucca trees. The quiet peace of the desert surrounded us.

"What's that?" said Cheryl as she jumped back, breaking the tranquility of the moment. A closer examination revealed a big ol' horny toad.

"What do you think would happen if we put that in Vicky's bed?" I mused.

The girls laughed, "Let's do it."

The thought of pulling a prank on Vicky delighted them. In a playful mood, I agreed. We slipped the frog into the house and hid it in my bathroom tub until bedtime. Vicky turned down her sheets and went into the bathroom.

"Quiet!" The girls couldn't keep from giggling. "Hold the sheets up," I said, "so I can slip this guy into the bottom of her bed."

Once the frog settled under the covers. I announced, "OK, girls, it's bedtime—lights out."

Vicky came out of the bathroom, and everyone pretended to say good night. But, instead, we hid around the corner of the hallway. We waited for Vicky to get into bed and turn off her light.

We held our breath.

"What the . . . " Vicky screamed, jumped out of bed, turned on the light, and ripped her bed apart. We flooded into her room in peals of laughter.

"What did you do!" she demanded as she continued searching her bed for the creature that had crawled up her leg. Finally, when the last blanket was removed, out jumped the toad, probably more scared than Vicky. She stared at it in disbelief and then broke into laughter.

"Good one, you guys! You scared me half to death!"

The girls couldn't stop laughing. The toad served his purpose and jumped off into the night while everyone tumbled into bed. These happy moments defused the more serious ones.

The most frightening incident occurred when I accepted a new girl named Peggy. She'd only been with us a week when I heard frantic pounding on my door. Upon opening it, the girls on the other side jumped up and down screaming, "She hurt herself!"

"Who? What happened?"

"Peggy! She's in the bathroom." I ran to the bathroom and found her with blood dripping down the front of her nightgown. She had cut her wrists and tried to slash her neck. It looked like a scene from a horror movie.

"Get some towels," I demanded. I grabbed the towels and wrapped them around Peggy's arm and neck to try and stop the bleeding.

"We've got to get her to the emergency room."

Terri wrapped her bathrobe around Peggy while I threw on my jeans, and we piled into the car.

"Vicky, keep those towels tight and her arms lifted." We raced down the highway to the hospital. When the emergency room nurse saw us, she hurried to help and immediately ushered Peggy into the doctor. He examined her and the deep cut on her wrist.

"The cut is so deep, I have to sew her vein before I can suture her wrist," he said. "Will you sit with her to distract her while I do this?"

"Of course." Being in the hospital brought much-needed relief. My greatest fear happened: a girl injured herself.

I sat beside Peggy and prayed under my breath while she laid on the table. I chatted about whatever popped into my mind to keep her attention away from the doctor. Her left wrist had the deepest wound, while her neck and right wrist were more superficial cuts.

"Okay, done," the doctor said. "You were a very good patient. Now we're going to transfer you back over to the psychiatric unit."

The doctor put her on a seventy-two-hour hold because of her suicide attempt. I walked her to the unit and hugged her goodbye as the nurse escorted her to her room. Exhaustion hit me as I drove home, but relief swept over me, knowing Peggy was safe in the hospital.

Then there were the usual everyday challenges. The girls planned a surprise birthday party for me. They invited a few friends, decorated the house with streamers, hung a Happy Birthday sign over the door with balloons, and made chocolate cupcakes. They worked hard to make the party special, and their sweetness touched my heart.

"These cupcakes are delicious," I said. "I'm saving this one for a special little treat tomorrow." I hid it in the refrigerator behind some leftovers.

The next day, all I could think about was the gooey chocolate frosting melting in my mouth for my last chocolate indulgence. I opened the refrigerator and couldn't find my cupcake. Loretta sat reading at the kitchen table.

"Loretta, did you see the cupcake that was in here?"

"I ate it," she said.

"You ate it?" I said. "Didn't you know it was for me?"

"Yes, I did."

157

"Then why did you eat it?"

"I wanted to."

"You ate it because you wanted to?" Okay, so much for my cupcake treat. I had to respect her honesty.

Loretta could never keep her thick black glasses clean or dandruff off her heavyset shoulders. She repetitively asked everyone she met, "Can I have a hug?" And everyone gave her a hug. She seemed to use this request to get attention. She caught me on an incredibly stressful day when she put her arms out with, "Can I have a hug?"

I replied, "No, Loretta, I'll give you a hug when I choose to give you a hug. Not when you keep asking for one."

She immediately backed away, "Okay."

After I finished my paperwork, I went to her room and said, "Do you still want a hug?"

She smiled. "Yes."

I gave her a big hug. "Loretta, I know you love to get hugs, but you have to be sensitive to other people."

"I know." But I didn't think she did.

"You need to let other people give you a hug. You can't keep asking them for one. That makes people feel uncomfortable."

"Okay."

"I didn't mean to hurt your feelings. Do you understand?"

She nodded and said, "Okay." She must have felt no one would offer her a hug unless she asked, and she was probably right, but I wanted her to learn how to be more appropriate with people.

Whoever thinks being a Christian is warming a pew somewhere like I did have never opened their hearts wide enough to enter the path where love becomes an adventure in living.

Chapter Eighteen:
Brown Bag Healing

TEARS OF RELEASE

The LORD is close to the brokenhearted
and saves those who are crushed in spirit.

Psalm 34:18

Karen sat motionless, staring out the chapel window. She sat for hours, like a breathing mass of pain. I sat next to her and tried to engage her in a conversation. If only I could reach inside and pull her from the hopelessness that shrouded her.

Her only movement was brushing the hair from her delicate facial features. Her petite frame made her appear younger than her twenty-eight years. I wanted to put my arms around her and tell her she would be all right.

"Sad isn't it," the nurse said as she came to take Karen to group therapy.

"What's her diagnosis?"

"Major depression with psychotic features. This is her third hospitalization."

Every day I sat with her, hoping she would speak. One day she said, "I feel cold and empty inside." Not to seem overly excited, I said, "I'm sorry, Karen. That must feel awful."

"Satan has control of my mind, and I can't think." Her insight startled me. "I don't feel anything."

"Those numb feelings can be part of the depression."

"I can't express myself, and I feel like an observer."

"I understand, Karen. You feel detached and disconnected."

"I don't care about anything anymore."

"When did this start?" I probed for more information.

"When my mother got upset because I stopped talking and watched TV all day. She sent me to the hospital."

"Did that help?" I hoped for something positive to build on.

"No, I didn't like it," she said. "My mother controlled me and took my kids."

"She took your kids?"

"Yeah, she put me in the hospital and filed for custody of my two kids from my first marriage."

"What about their father?"

"He left us for another woman, and no one knows where he is."

There were times when certain people pulled on my heartstrings more than others. Those are the ones I know God is connecting me with for a particular reason.

When the time came for her to be discharged, the hospital aftercare recommended an alternative placement. They didn't think returning her back to her mother would be helpful and asked if I would take her. Karen hesitated and kept saying, "I don't feel anything. I am numb inside."

"I know, but keep putting God first. He will help you connect with your feelings."

When we arrived at the house, the girls welcomed her and helped her adjust. Karen showed up for the house activities, attended church, listened to the Bible studies, and continued her weekly psychiatric appointments. She remained detached and rarely communicated until she gradually emerged from her isolation.

We sat on the swing in the backyard and I asked her, "How did you get to the point where you needed hospitalization?"

"I got pregnant at sixteen and married the guy," she said. "We had two kids before I couldn't take it anymore."

"Was he abusive?"

"Sometimes, but his other women hurt the most. After I filed for divorce, I found out I was pregnant."

"Did you tell your husband?"

"No. I married his friend, and everyone thought the baby was his."

"So, your ex-husband never knew?"

"No, his friend is the father listed on the birth certificate. That's why he's petitioning for full custody after the divorce."

"And that's why your mother got custody of your first two kids? Because their father wasn't around, and your current husband kept the youngest?

She looked at the ground and pushed the swing back with her foot.

"I know this is difficult, but have you forgiven your mother and husbands?"

"What difference does it make? I can't feel anything anyway."

"When we forgive, we're aligning with God's will and allowing him to help us." I knew God would honor even her feeblest efforts.

"I suppose," she responded. I led her through a prayer of forgiveness. At least this was a start.

Several weeks passed, and the date to sign the final divorce papers approached.

"Pam, when am I going to feel something?"

"I don't know. We have to trust God's timing."

"I don't even feel anything when I hold my baby."

"Trying to stifle painful feelings can shut down the entire emotional system, including the ability to feel love," I explained. Her numbness revealed a world of hidden pain inside. I prayed with her and asked God, again, to help her connect with her feelings.

A few days later, I left to do the weekly grocery shopping. When I returned, I found Karen sitting on the floor in the middle of the den with a large brown grocery bag in front of her overflowing with soggy Kleenex. The girls surrounded her and were trying to comfort her.

When they saw me, they jumped up and said, "She's been crying ever since you left!"

"What happened?"

"Her husband called about the divorce," Vicky said.

I took the groceries into the kitchen and went back to sit with her.

"My husband wants a divorce!" She sounded like she heard it for the first time. "The divorce will be final this month!" I put my arms around her and rocked her like a bawling child. After a few minutes, her crying subsided into intermittent sniffles.

"Well, I guess you got in touch with your feelings, didn't you." She gave me a shy smile and blew her nose.

"Did I do that?" she said, pointing to the brown bag filled with wet tissues.

"Yep, that's the pain you had locked inside." I handed her another tissue. Her tears drenched the front of her shirt, and her eyes were swollen slits. The painful truth of her pending divorce and the potential loss of her child finally registered, and she connected to her grief.

After she stopped crying, I said, "Feeling better?"

She nodded as she wiped her nose.

"Oh, man, where did that come from?" she said. I touched her stomach, indicating, "Way down there."

The breakthrough arrived, and for the first time, we heard Karen laugh. The call from her husband must have been the last straw that cracked the wall barricading her emotions and opened the floodgates.

Once Karen relaxed, she said, "I don't know what happened, Pam, but after that meltdown, I'm not as numb anymore." Her eyes twinkled. I smiled at the good news.

"Jesus answered our prayers, didn't he?" she said. "I haven't ever felt this good." She lifted her hand to acknowledge him. Her beautiful face glowed. "I'll trust him with the divorce. Whatever happens, is up to him." I gave her a big hug.

The following week, her husband picked her up. They planned to spend the day with her daughter before meeting with the attorney. The day dragged by as I prayed and waited to find out the results of her meeting.

When I heard the car pull into the driveway, I went to meet her. She and her husband came in with their sleeping daughter.

"How did it go?" I asked. Karen smiled and gave me a big hug.

"You'll never believe what happened," she said. "All we did was talk . . ."

"I can't believe the change in her," her husband interrupted. "She's a different person." The hour drive to the city gave Karen time to share her breakthrough with her husband. "When I saw her with our daughter, I knew I still loved her and wanted my family back."

"We never made it to the divorce attorney," Karen said, and they started giggling like teenagers, stumbling over each other's words.

"We canceled the divorce," he said, "and if things keep working out . . ."

"We're going to renew our wedding vows!" she gushed.

"Yes, and after that, we're going to get the kids from her mother."

"Wow! All that in one afternoon?" I couldn't believe this miracle. "When God does something, He really does it—doesn't He?" The joy on her face erased my first image of her sitting isolated on the psychiatric unit. "I'm thrilled for both of you."

The girls gathered around and congratulated them with lots of hugs.

God is never too early, or too late, but right on time. He honored our prayers and intervened in the nick of time. "He has made everything beautiful in its time.[19]"

THE FREEDOM
OF
LIBERATION

Chapter Nineteen:
Returning to Egypt

PREPARED FOR A PURPOSE

*Therefore, if anyone is in Christ, the new creation has come: The
old has gone, the new is here!*

2 Corinthians 5:17

"The Vineyard is planning a trip to the Holy Land," Janis said,
"I'd really like to go. Can you get away?" Janis, who had
traveled with me to Rome before we were saved, started
attending the church shortly after I did.

"I'd love to go." The thought of reconnecting with Pastor Kenn and
my LA friends excited me. "Let me see what I can work out." Walking
where Jesus walked and sharing that experience with my spiritual family
sounded like a little bit of heaven.

The girls were stable and could manage the household routines. It
might work.

Frank knew the girls, and I trusted him, so I called and asked, "If I
left for a couple of weeks, could you oversee the house and make sure
the girls are okay?"

"Sure, not a problem," he responded.

That settled it. My first break in over two years would be a trip to
Israel.

The time in Israel took me back to those historic Biblical times, and
the life of Christ took on a new realism. My pastor, Kenn, and John
Wimber[20] taught at pivotal places and expounded on their scriptural
relevance. This ancient world ignited my curiosity to explore the shops
and culture. I didn't want to miss any of it.

"Pam, how would you like to take a walk with me?" Kenn said, "I'd
like to visit the Knesset."

"Great!" I responded, adding, "We have a lot to catch up on."

During our leisurely stroll, I chattered incessantly about the miracles I had witnessed at the hospital and how God moved in the most impossible situations. My obvious enthusiasm about the Christian Therapy Program intrigued him.

"Pam, we have a lot of people coming to the church from the entertainment industry. Many have issues with drugs and alcohol that our pastoral staff is not prepared to deal with. Would you consider helping us?"

This shifted the conversation in an unexpected direction.

"Would you consider joining our staff in West Los Angeles?" he said.

"Leave Lancaster and move back to LA?"

"Yes, I suppose so."

Here we go again—every time I started to settle into a place, the Lord had a way of uprooting me. My work with the hospital earned me credits towards my doctoral degree in ministry. The training I received provided tangible, pragmatic, and relevant answers that taught me how to apply the Word of God to various complex situations.

The desert simplified my life and freed me from the superficial vanity of Hollywood. I believe God sent me to the desert to discover his oasis of healing through the Christian Therapy Program. I experienced how the principles of scripture came to life in a powerful, professional way with miraculous results.

Leaving the security of this team would be difficult. I would not have the hospital's professional resources, or the ability to collaborate with doctors, or have a nursing staff monitor behaviors or treatment team meetings. I wouldn't have access to the wisdom of my clinical mentors.

Bringing this knowledge into a church setting where no one understood therapeutic interventions would be a challenge. Why did God lead me into situations beyond my abilities? He continually taught me to be dependent on him.

After returning from Israel, I made an appointment with Kenn to discuss the move.

"I'm not sure I can come on staff full time," I said. "The girls still need oversight." They were thriving but still needed accountability. If I took on this challenge, I wanted the support of the Christian Therapy Program. They would help me be more effective at the Vineyard.

"What if I work four days at the Vineyard and three days in Lancaster?

It wasn't ideal, but Kenn agreed.

As hard as leaving Los Angeles had been, moving back created a different set of fears. Returning to the city reminded me of going back to Egypt. Moses didn't relish returning to Egypt and balked at the idea, "Lord, please![21] Send anyone else." But when God calls you out of the desert, it's because he's prepared you for a purpose. God knows you are ready for what *he* wants to accomplish.

I didn't want to be seduced back into the Hollywood scene with all its materialism and pride. God often takes us out of a situation to purify our hearts before he brings us back. Once free, we are more useful for kingdom purposes, "when the Son sets you free[22], you are free indeed." Could I withstand the worldly seductions? I was about to find out.

I started on staff at the Vineyard and began to utilize what I learned at the hospital to apply the word of God. I provided individual counseling while I developed leadership training and personal growth groups. I also persuaded Frank to come down from the hospital to help me facilitate marriage groups. The demand for healing was tremendous.

Without Kenn's support in those early days of transition, I might have crumbled under the weight of my responsibilities. Several Vineyard churches throughout Southern California requested leadership training once they heard how God was moving in people's lives.

The apostle Paul had a mission to share what he learned with those who could teach others. "The things you have heard[23] me say in the presence of many witnesses entrust to reliable people who will also be qualified to teach others."

I certainly didn't equate myself to the apostle Paul, but I knew God brought me back to Los Angeles to teach others the deeper principles of inner healing. I couldn't believe the hunger in the body of Christ for these answers—the same answers I hungered for in my life.

The grace of God and gallons of coffee sustained me with my crazy schedule. Returning to the desert and the hospital became my only respite.

The staff at John Wimber's church in Yorba Linda invited me to run a group. The thought made me nervous. I had great respect for John and his staff and wondered, *Who am I to teach these gifted men and women of God? I had to remind myself, just share what God taught you and leave the results to him.*

John's appearance reminded me of what I thought Moses might look like: A large, rotund man with white hair and beard and twinkling eyes full of wisdom. He glowed with what the church considered his apostolic anointing[24] and effortless style. God moved supernaturally through the Vineyard churches in Southern California. John and his staff witnessed powerful gifts of physical healing, and Lonnie Frisbee[25] ignited an extraordinary move of the Holy Spirit that caught fire in the church. As a result, John began developing a course on signs and wonders for Fuller Seminary.

The Vineyard burst forth[26] from its seedling vision initially planted in Kenn Gulliksen's heart. A former Calvary Chapel pastor, Kenn set out to pioneer the first Vineyard church plant in New Mexico and grow churches throughout the United States. His West LA church plant is where I received salvation and returned to become part of their staff several years later. Many Calvary Chapel pastors migrated over to Kenn's vision for the Vineyards, John Wimber[27] being one of them.

John had managed the Righteous Brothers and played keyboard himself. He and Kenn revolutionized worship with other gifted worship leaders, and the small group of churches known as the Vineyard Christian Fellowship grew into an international Vineyard[28] movement.

Lonnie Frisbee, a radical hippy leader in the Jesus People movement, joined John in Anaheim and released supernatural signs and wonders. I joined Kenn in Los Angeles and pioneered an in-depth integrative approach to inner healing. Together these mighty moves of God drew people from all walks of life, including the entertainment and music business. As a result, the Vineyard exploded with love and vitality for Jesus.

God's magnificence was radically poured out, and his tender mercies enveloped each service. People streamed in for a touch of his love and a new revelation of God's reality.

Famous entertainers and celebrities regularly attended church services. Singers like Johnny Rivers, Bob Dylan, and his guitarist—T Bone Burnett, Donna Summer—the Queen of Disco, contemporary Christian music pioneer Keith Green, Debbie Boone and spouse—Gabriel Ferrar.

Award-winning songwriter/composer Al Kasha led a Bible study for those in the entertainment industry. Many would become successful Hollywood producers. Peter Engel created the TV series *Saved by the Bell*. Terry Botwick produced *Captive* based on the true story of how the book *Purpose Driven Life* saved a convict's life, and Tony Eldridge produced *The Equalizer*.

Other notables attended regularly like singer/songwriter Jamie Collen Owens, Wendell Burton, who starred opposite Lisa Minnelli in the *Sterile Cuckoo*, and Jerry Houser of the *Summer of '42* movie, to name a few.

This sovereign move of God released contagious joy. This was no austere religious experience but a river of living water for our thirsty souls. This dynamic expression of God's love transformed lives.

I met Susan Muneo, Donna Summer's manager, when I attended Al Kasha's Bible study. Our friendship grew, and I enjoyed getting to know Donna and Susan's family and friends.

My interaction with the entertainment industry changed. I finally found my purpose. God gave me a passion for the broken-hearted and seeing lives restored to Christ. I'm as comfortable sitting with a street kid in the squats as I am sitting in the mansions of the rich and famous. Because God looked at my heart with love and acceptance, I can model that same acceptance for others. The freedom I experienced gives me eyes to see through the masks without judgment.

*Attending Donna Summer's record release party
with Donna and her sister Linda*

With the late, great Lonnie Frisbee

My time with Kenn at the Vineyard allowed me to participate in several church plants including Santa Monica, Newport Beach, and a summer in Massachusetts in preparation for Kenn's eventual move home to Boston. In addition, Kenn and Joanie took me into their family. Their gentle spirits, profound wisdom, and tender care for their children inspired me, and my more high-spirited personality was tempered through their kindness.

We traveled to Africa, Israel, England, Norway, Denmark, Rome, Greece, and other parts of the world on ministry trips. I enjoyed watching their adorable children grow into amazing adults. Not only was I saved through Kenn's ministry, but they personally nurtured me as a spiritual child, released me to grow, and gave wings to my gifting. Their shining example of Christian love shaped my dedication to Christ.

Kenn released the Santa Monica Vineyard over to Jim Kermath, his associate pastor, and started his last church plant in Newport before leaving the west coast. His vision was to return to his beloved Massachusetts and plant a church.

As for me, I trained several health care providers in the Santa Monica church before I left, and they went on to receive their PhDs, stayed at the church, and formed a non-profit organization that carried on the counseling work.

One day a week, I drove to Newport to establish the counseling program for Kenn. I developed the foundation and was surprised when Kenn said, "The church is growing so fast I think we need a full-time person to oversee the counseling program. Would you consider coming on full time?"

"I agree the program could use someone full-time, but I'm not sure I am up to it." I didn't have much energy left after five years of intense ministry and didn't think I could manage driving every day to Newport.

"There is a psychiatrist in our church that is interested. Can you meet with him?"

I met with him, and although he and I didn't agree on some things, Kenn brought him on board. I laid the groundwork, got the program up and running, and could now pass it on to a full-time person.

While Kenn and the family planned their move back to Massachusetts, God led me in another direction. Our time in ministry together may have come to an end, but our history and friendship never would.

My friendship with Susan Muneo continued to grow. She and her clients attended Church on the Way (COTW) in Van Nuys, so it became a natural transition for me to attend their church. COTW formed the biblical foundation for the Christian Therapy Program, and many of Pastor Jack Hayford's teachings were foundational to the Bible studies taught at the hospital. Dr. Nichols, his wife, and Dr. Gross attended COTW and were close friends with Pastor Jack before he became an internationally recognized minister. In Addition, I enjoyed the anonymity of being in a church where I didn't have a staff position. It allowed me a new sense of freedom.

During these foundational years of ministry, I plowed non-stop into new territories and fought battles for those who weren't strong enough to fight for themselves while trying to stay on top of my own healing. Being forged in the refining fires of ministry certainly made me stronger. The betrayals I encountered brought God's grace closer, and the rejections I suffered tested my faith, while the joy of seeing lives pulled from despair branded my heart with God's love.

During this transition time, I took a refresher class at L.I.F.E. Bible College in Echo Park to refuel my depleted spirit. I loved being a student.

During one of my classes, the instructor said, "Let's take the rest of our time to intercede for the missionaries in Third World countries."

I looked at my watch. *That's over an hour*, said my inner critic. While another voice piped up, *Oh, no! I think you're in big trouble.* This started an internal conflict. One voice recognized my resistance to praying, and the other voice didn't care.

I don't want to talk to Jesus, said the petulant voice.

Pam, what is wrong with you?

I don't know what's wrong. I just don't have anything to say.

How can you not have anything to say to Jesus?

My resistance grew more defiant. I wouldn't open my mouth to pray. I just knelt in front of my chair with my head buried in my hands, and my heart hardened.

What is wrong with you?

Then it hit me—the revelation of what was blocking my desire to pray: *Jesus and pain had become synonymous.*

My entire history in ministry with all the misunderstandings, hurts, rejections, and disappointments, came flooding to the surface like a flash flood barreling down a canyon. The tears began to flow as the lump in my throat thickened.

I heaved sobs of grief as I hid my face. I didn't want to look around for fear of what others might think. *Maybe they'll think I'm in deep intercession.* That thought fizzled when I felt someone's hand on my back. I wanted to shout, "Go away—leave me alone." Soon the hand lifted off my back.

It felt like someone cut through my calloused heart, and I couldn't stop the bleeding. "What's wrong with me? Jesus, you know I love you."

How could Jesus and pain be synonymous? *I served you all these years and dealt with these hurts. . . . They're in the past. So where is this coming from?*

For three days, I woke up crying. When I went to class, tears streamed down my face. I pulled over driving home because I couldn't see through my tears. I ate soggy food drenched in tears. I couldn't stop crying! Finally, I called my friend, John, who served on staff with me at the Vineyard before moving to Annapolis, Maryland, to plant a Vineyard.

"John, I can't stop crying. I don't know what is wrong with me."

I didn't understand John's response when he said, "Pam, the Spirit of the Lord is all over you."

"Really? It sure doesn't feel like it." I continued to cry. John prayed for me, and I had a brief moment of peace.

Buried deep in my heart under all my theology and "Christianese," I had a childish, idealistic expectation of Jesus. I believed he would wave his magic wand and make everything perfect. Just like I thought years ago about having a Crisis house ministry where we would bake bread, hang chintz curtains, and Jesus would heal everyone. But, instead, Jesus told me back then to "count the cost," and I balked, not understanding.

Salvation is not some cheap grace; it's about transformation and restoration. "And since we are his children[29], we will share his treasures—for all God gives to his Son Jesus is now ours too. But if we are to share his glory, we must also share his suffering."

I gave Jesus my heart in childlike innocence and pursued him with complete abandonment, but then the disillusionments came: the bread burnt, the chintz curtains were torn, and not everyone was healed. The ache in my heart returned along with the tears. I remembered the friends I trusted who talked behind my back, the mentors I looked up to who disappointed me, the people I cared about who used me for their own advantage, and the people who only called me when they needed something. I poured myself out selflessly, only to be used, misunderstood, and betrayed.

"But I've forgiven them, Lord. I forgave them back then."

Most people only saw the strength of my anointing, but they didn't see me. They didn't see the child inside struggling with her own fears and insecurities. They never understand how much they hurt her. Maybe I kept my vulnerabilities too well hidden, or they never looked close enough, or perhaps they just couldn't see beyond their own needs.

Being in leadership made it difficult to find the time to thoroughly process my hurts. I did my best to forgive when they happened, but life gets in the way, and the needs of others take precedence. God, in his mercy, must have decided I needed a little extra help. His Holy Spirit began to Roto-Rooter my clogged emotional plumbing. I didn't understand how much residue from past hurts still remained or the pain they carried. Deep calls to deep, and the Lord moved into the deepest parts of my soul.

As incidents and people came to mind, I asked the Lord to show me any remaining pain or resentment I needed to forgive. After forgiving them, I released that person to the Lord and asked God to bless them. As he purged the emotional gangrene, his forgiveness cauterized the wounds and left no visible scar. To my astonishment, his gentle love poured over me and tenderized the hardened places of my heart.

Little by little, the tears subsided, and a new freshness replaced the stagnation. My heart vibrated with a radiant love for Jesus. He saw every hurt and injustice I suffered and brought healing to my soul. I felt new freedom as tears of joy rolled down my cheeks in gratitude. He turned my past sufferings into a beautiful intimacy, drawing me deeper into his loving embrace.

"Lord, I love you more than words can say. I would go through everything again just to know you like I do right now. I would do it all again."

God, I invite your searching gaze into my heart.
Examine me through and through;
Find out everything that may be hidden within me...
See if there is any path of pain I'm walking on,
And lead me back to your glorious, everlasting ways —

Psalm 139:23-24 TPT

Chapter Twenty:
Doing It All Again

HOMES OF HOPE

*God is the only one who can make
the Valley of Trouble, a door of hope.*

Catherine Marshall (based on Hosea 2:15)

*May the God of hope fill you with all joy and peace, as you trust
in him, so that you may overflow with hope by the power of the
Holy Spirit.*

Romans 15:13

"I've decided to sell the Christian Therapy Program to Steve Arterburn of New Life," announced Dr. Gross to a few of us seated in his office. "He's going to franchise it into multiple hospitals to serve the Christian community." There were rumblings of this, but the reality unsettled me.

Dr. Gross had expanded the program to the Buena Park Community Hospital, where I functioned as a group facilitator while completing my master's in marriage and family counseling at the California Christian Institute in Orange County. The hospital program taught me the fundamentals of Christian therapy and became my family. The staff functioned as a team, and we supported each other. I wondered how the absence of Dr. Gross would affect the direction of the program.

On top of my already hectic schedule, I agreed to be the executive director for Homes of Hope, a discipleship program for the street kids in Hollywood. This addition wouldn't be easy, but the kids had my heart. Just a few months earlier, I told God *I would do it all again*. And here I am—right back where I started! God brought me full circle but this time, better prepared.

My cathartic release of emotions at L.I.F.E. Bible College cleared the emotional residue of my past season in ministry and paved the way for this fresh new season. I understood the importance of the lessons I learned. Every difficulty I overcame gave me courage. Every hardship I endured built inner strength. Every disappointment I suffered taught me forgiveness, and every loss I incurred gave way to greater freedom. He developed determination in my life and replaced my childish expectations with a more mature understanding of the spiritual battles in life.

"Friends, when life gets really difficult[30], don't jump to the conclusion that God isn't on the job. Instead, be glad that you are in the very thick of what Christ experienced. This is a spiritual refining process, with glory just around the corner" (1 Peter 4: 12–13 MSG).

My trust in God's goodness deepened, and I hope, above all, God saw he could trust me to always put him first.

Homes of Hope, located miles from the Hollywood Street scene, provided a quiet residential environment. The house was comfortable with three bedrooms, two bathrooms, a dining room, a comfortable living room, and a large open room in the back of the house that served as a small dormitory. We had a nice backyard and garage. It met all our needs.

Judy Radachy, director of the Oasis of Hollywood, sat on my board of directors and became a great friend. The Oasis provided a Christian club in Hollywood that drew in the kids from the streets. The girls at the house continued some of their friendships with those not ready to come off the streets. They reached out to them when they were at the Oasis and encouraged them to accept Jesus.

While sitting in the living room after dinner, the girls surrounded me. "Okay, what's up?" I said, "You guys are up to something. What is it?" They giggled and explained their idea.

"Can we have a B.B.Q. and invite our friends?" Jennifer said. Their friends were the kids still living on the streets.

"What a great idea." Their initiative touched me. "Ask them to bring their clothes. They can shower and do laundry while we B.B.Q.," I said. "How does that sound?"

Their faces lit up. "I'll even send the station wagon to pick them up."

They gave me hugs and thanked me before running off to make plans.

Word traveled fast on the streets, and on the day of the B.B.Q., it took three trips to pick up all the kids. When the first car pulled up, the most ragtag, tough-looking punkers you could imagine climbed out. Some had spiked green hair and wore black dog collars around their necks. The girls wore black Goth eye makeup and short skirts. Others had scuffed leather motorcycle boots and grungy, smelly clothes from living in the squats, the abandoned buildings where the kids slept. Luckily the neighbors didn't call the police when they saw them arriving.

"Hi, guys," Regina said as they sauntered into the house, "You can take a shower over there." She pointed to the bathroom. "Here's a towel, and there's soap and shampoo already in there."

"Hand your clothes out to us, and we'll wash them," Jennifer said, "Here's a pair of sweatpants and a t-shirt to wear." The girls had stacked up towels and donated their sweatpants and t-shirts.

I marveled when the girls emerged from the showers. Without all the street camouflage and their tough exteriors washed away, they looked like typical teenagers. The girls kept the washing machine humming, folded their clothes, and invited their guests to the backyard feast of burgers and hot dogs.

"I'll unwrap the cookies," Tammy said, then directed the other girls, "Lay the bread on the counter; it'll be faster to make the sandwiches." They had a little assembly line set up in the kitchen.

"Here are the paper bags," Jennifer said, "two sandwiches, an apple, and some cookies, right?"

"I found a box to put the to-go lunches in," Regina said. "They can each take a bag when they leave."

I watched in admiration as they worked together.

Our backyard turned into a playground of laughter. The kids took turns shooting hoops; others sat in small groups talking and eating, while several wandered over and said, "Thank you for letting us come. This is really nice of you."

I walked into the house and noticed a girl sitting alone on the couch. She looked fragile and younger than the rest. I introduced myself and found out her name was Julie. She ran away from her foster home and had been on the streets since she turned fifteen.

"Why were you placed in a foster home?"

Julie lowered her eyes and stopped eating. I waited.

"My mom's in prison."

"I'm sorry, Julie. What happened?"

"It's a long story."

"I have time." She hesitated. Her eyes narrowed as she assessed me.

"My step-dad molested me when I was twelve. I told my mom, and she pressed charges, and they sent him to prison."

"Your mom did the right thing."

"Yeah, well, she blamed herself for what happened and felt so guilty she went back on drugs." She slammed her plate on the table. "They busted her and sent her to prison and sent me to a foster home." She shot off the couch. "It's my fault. I shouldn't have told her."

"Julie, you had to tell your mother." I extended my hand, but she turned away. "What your stepfather did was wrong. Your mom loved you and wanted to protect you."

"Right, and now she's in prison." She glared at me.

"Would you rather have her be in prison or dead from an overdose?"

Her glare turned to confusion, "What are you talking about?" She sat down.

"Do you think maybe God is protecting her from herself right now? She's off drugs and has time to process what happened."

"I never thought about it like that."

"Julie, I can't imagine how hard this must be." She nodded her head. "Your mom loves you, and I believe God can make a way for you to be together again."

"You think so?" A glimmer of hope appeared.

"Yes, I really do. Can I pray for you and your mom?" Julie took my hands, and we prayed. "Lord, have mercy on Julie and her mother. Heal their pain and make a way for them to be united. Give Julie peace and keep them both safe." I gave her a hug. "Would you like to stay here with us?"

"I'm not sure. Can I think about it?" I knew that meant no. Even as tough as the streets can be, they are often safer than other places these kids have been.

The Church on the Way offered their beautiful auditorium for a fundraiser for Homes of Hope. Lisa Whelchel, who played Blair on *The Facts of Life*, a popular 80s sitcom, offered to play with her band on one condition—I would take her to the streets and introduce her to the kids. That would be easy to make happen. Lisa and I had met while attending the Vineyard together.

At dinner that evening, I told the girls, "Guess who's coming for dinner next Friday?" I had their attention. "Lisa Whelchel."

"Are you kidding us?" The thought of meeting one of their favorite TV stars excited them.

"She wants to meet you." I said, "After dinner, we're going to the Oasis before we go out on the streets."

"Can we come too?" Jennifer said.

"You can come to the Oasis, but you'll have to wait there while we go meet the kids."

Regina cleared the table. "What do you think she'll be like?"

"She's so pretty," Jennifer said, "Do you think she'll like us?"

"That's so cool that Lisa wants to meet the kids on the streets. I can't believe she's coming here for dinner."

The girls bustled around all day cleaning, making dinner, arranging flowers for the table, and making everything perfect for their special guest.

"She's here!" came a shout. The girls ran to the door.

"Hi, Lisa," I said. "Welcome. Everyone is anxious to meet you." The girls gathered around her.

"I've been looking forward to meeting you," Lisa said with a smile. "Tell me your names." She jumped right in. After the introductions, the girls became little chatterboxes, asking questions and sharing stories that made Lisa laugh.

Chris (Amii's son), Lisa, Amii and girls

Lisa and I met Ron and Judy at the Oasis before I took Lisa to meet the kids on the streets. It was a fun night for all.

After dinner, I said, "Okay, it's time to go." We piled into the car and headed to the Oasis. Judy and her husband, Ron, met us and showed Lisa around their building, and explained the resources they provided for the kids.

"The kids hang out at a burger place on Santa Monica Boulevard, so let's start there," I said.

We arrived at the place jam-packed with a vast array of characters. Bruce, a street kid, came over. "Hey, Pam, what are you doing here?"

"I'm here with my friend, Lisa."

"Wait . . . are you that girl from *The Facts of Life?*"

Lisa smiled and said, "Yes, that's me."

Bruce's face lit up, and he called his friends over as we sat down.

Soon the table filled with kids. Lisa's plucky personality delighted them as they laughed and joked with her. Her effortless way of interacting showed no signs of apprehension.

The night of the big fundraiser arrived. Hundreds of people packed the auditorium to overflowing. After Jennifer and Pam, two girls from our house shared their stories, I had a big surprise for everyone.

"I don't know if I can do this," Jennifer said, "I've never done this before." I grabbed her clammy hands and said, "You're going to do great. I'll be right there with you, and so will Jesus."

Pam kept wringing her hands, and her pretty face turned ashen, "You promise you'll help us if we mess up?"

"Of course, but you're not going to mess up," I said. "The fact that you're here is already a victory." I gave them both a hug, and we prayed together. "Talk from your heart, and Jesus will do the rest."

185

Pam   *Me*   *Jennifer*

Lisa addressing the audience

After Lisa and her band finished their rousing performance, I brought Jennifer and Pam to the platform. Pam shared how her schizophrenic mother abused her and why she ran away from fourteen different foster homes. Pam went to New York, where two of her friends were murdered from street gang violence. In fear for her life, she hopped a bus to Hollywood to get as far away from New York as possible. Soon after arriving, she was beaten and raped, which led her to Homes of Hope.

Jennifer, an indigenous teen, shared how she ran away from the people she lived with at thirteen. She talked about life on the streets and how she started using drugs and became addicted. She found a new life through Christ. The packed sanctuary sat in hushed silence as they recounted their painful histories. Hearing how God intervened and rescued these young lives from their dangerous circumstances revealed God's ever-present help in times of trouble.

The girls left the stage.

"Is Pastor Jack here?" I said.

"I'm here, Pam." He came to the platform with a puzzled look on his face since I extemporaneously inserted this in the agenda.

"This afternoon, I received a telegram I would love for you to read." I took the telegram from its hiding place in my pocket and handed it to Pastor Jack. Not knowing what it said, he took a minute to scan its contents.

I turned to the right, holding the microphone to acknowledge the audience. Then, ready to read it, Pastor Jack had no microphone, making the audience chuckle. When I noticed, I handed him the mic.

"Sorry . . . here you go."

"Thank you, Pam." The audience laughed. He read the telegram:

THE WHITE HOUSE

WASHINGTON

February 26, 1988

The Reverend Donn Moomaw has told me that you're celebrating your first anniversary. Congratulations!

Your truly special ministry offers loving homes, as well as counseling and vocational education, to homeless young women who are looking for a way to change their lives. Thanks to you, many have been able to make a fresh start. I can think of no finer service than the faith, the strength and support, and the love you provide to young women who might otherwise have concluded they had nowhere left to turn.

Again, congratulations. Nancy and I pray that your work will flourish, and we send best wishes for many more anniversaries. God bless you and everyone you serve.

Ronald Reagan

Pam and Pastor Jack Hayford of Church on the Way

After reading the telegram Pastor Jack paused, lifted his head, and with a broad smile, he proudly announced, "Ronald Reagan."

The audience roared with appreciation and stunned my Board of Directors. God honored our work with this humbling word of encouragement. As Scripture promises, "Seek first the kingdom[31] of God and all else will be added unto you… exceedingly abundantly above all that we ask or think . . . for love never fails."

The presence, power, and faithfulness of God were on full display that glorious night.

Those shaky first steps of obedience that lead me into the crisis house in Hollywood opened my heart to the needs of hurting humanity. My sojourn into the desert taught me additional skills to facilitate the healing process. My years on staff at the Vineyard gave me the courage to impart this knowledge to others, and Homes of Hope brought everything full circle.

I did not understand when I took my first step of faith where God would lead me. Despite the outcries of my flesh, I continued to surrender. I pursued his will for my life, and he continued to reveal himself. Step by step, I learned to trust him as he proved himself faithful. He accepted me with all my flaws and fears.

As I continued to follow him, he not only restored my life but also allowed me the privilege of helping others restore their lives. We comfort others out of the comfort we have received (2 Corinthians 1:3–5).

"Many are called[32] but few are chosen." I am humbled God called me and thankful that I found the courage to say, "Yes, Lord, thy will be done—not mine."

Kids and volunteers from Homes of Hope thanking the president

EPILOGUE

New Life bought the Dr. Fred Gross Christian Therapy Hospital Program, and everything continued as usual. No one lost their jobs, and our clinical family stayed the same.

"Pam, New Life wants to open a program in Van Nuys," the marketing director said. "Why don't you apply for the program director position?"

"What?" I just received my master's in marriage and family counseling and didn't have the strength to take on the responsibility of administering a new program. I enjoyed being part of a team—not creating a team. I loved being a group leader, not an administrator.

"No one knows the program like you. You'd do a great job."

"Let me think about it, and we can talk later."

After prayer and consideration, I agreed to an interview with the hospital administrator. Perhaps I could give other clinicians the same opportunity given to me.

I marveled at all God had brought me through. I received salvation at the Vineyard and several years later returned to become part of the staff. I started a crisis house in Hollywood as a young Christian, knowing nothing, and returned several years later to be the director of Homes of Hope. I went to the desert to start a home that became a mental health rehabilitation home, joined a hospital staff, received my doctorate degree and a master's degree, and now had the opportunity to replicate a program that would impart to others the principles of healing. Full circle—again. There is a purpose in everything God does in our lives.

I accepted this new challenge as program director and developed a staff and program that scored 98% on the patient satisfaction survey. As program director, my years with Dr. Gross and my wonderful clinical mentors brought closure to that part of my life. I was able to give back to others what had been given to me.

Over time, hospital stays became shorter due to insurance, and the inpatient programs were phased out for less expensive forms of care. After leaving my position as program director, I went on to establish my private practice.

I'm grateful for every experience that transformed my life, including the painful ones. Every step drew me closer to God and gave me greater confidence in his ability to fashion something beautiful out of all my mistakes and hardships.

Rick Warren, the author of the #1 *New York Times* Bestseller *The Purpose Driven Life*, starts out by saying, "It's not about you." I believe that is true—but let me pose another point of view. What if "it is about you?" God never violates our free will. So, it is about *you* and how much you're willing to surrender in pursuit of God's purpose for your life. When the road gets rough, will I continue to walk with him? When I don't understand what he is doing, will I choose to trust him? Will I fight through the pain, fear, anger, and doubt to reach his heart and learn his ways?

There is an adventure into the spiritual realm unique for each person. Your story will be different from mine because we all have different callings, gifts, and purposes. I challenge you to step out of your safety zone and ask God to show you the truth about who he wants to be *to you* and *through you!* You have a destiny and purpose to fulfill in this life.

At eighteen, I won a crown that changed my life. I tarnished that crown by compromising my values and losing myself in the process. Following after the world's system corroded the truth and drained me of my joy for living.

Then God met me at the crossroads of my life and began to restore what I lost. He gave me a new heart and a new life, full of joy and purpose. I persevered through the trials and allowed him to have his way in my life. I fell more in love with him as I pressed through to gain his truth. Through the process, I found the freedom to celebrate the life he gave me; God promises a crown of life to those who love him. I love him more than life itself. The pain he suffered because of his great love for me is excruciatingly beautiful. Once that revelation shatters your heart, your only desire is to be near him. I *know* God loves me. The knowing I have is not just a Christian cliché. It is a deep knowing in my soul that comes with experience and can never be taken away. Life may challenge me, people may disappoint me, I may face loss and adversity, but the comfort of God will never abandon me. That is the truth that heals. This is the love that restores the soul.

Is your crown tarnished? Why not let God replace it with a new eternal crown? There's one waiting just for you. He rewards those who seek him with so much more than you could ever imagine.

Lord, bless each person who reads these words. Draw them into the beauty of your love. Reveal your truth and reality to them. Be a tangible and undeniable presence in their life, and bring them comfort. Help them find the authenticity of who you created them to be and their unique purpose in this life. Let your love pour over them and give them peace. Amen.

For those who don't know God or his beautiful son, Jesus, and would like to, all you have to do is ask him to come into your heart and make you new:

Lord Jesus, please forgive me for all my mistakes and sins. I believe you are real and rose from the dead that I might be restored to eternal life through your shed blood on the cross. You are the only begotten son of God. Help me, Lord, to grow in truth. Thank you for your unconditional love for me. I surrender my life to you. Amen.

ABOUT THE COVER ARTIST

Kenn Gulliksen is a man of many talents. He originally wanted to be an architect, but God had different plans. Instead, he founded the Vineyard Christian Fellowship as a non-denominational church that eventually grew into an internationally recognized denomination.

Kenn painted a series of watercolors from a collection of photos taken in Massachusetts the summer we returned from a ministry trip to South Africa. I stayed with Kenn and his family that summer as he prepared the way for a new church plant later that year.

Kenn gifted me with his original watercolor when I received my Master's in Marriage and Family counseling. When asked why he chose to paint this particular photo he said:

As we were sailing to New Bedford from Martha's Vineyard, the simple, powerful beauty of the seascape, and the powerful lines of the composition overwhelmed me. The colors were fantastic—the rich blues of the sky and sea, balanced by the striking red of Pam's outfit and off white of the ship.

But what drew me most was seeing my beloved friend and sister in the Lord simply being quiet, basking in the sweet grace of God surrounded by his tranquil peace. Pam was normally surrounded by the needs of others, bringing healing to their sufferings as she held them in her arms and prayed for them. Today, her compassionate best friend, Jesus, was embracing her. I could feel his tender love and calm resting on her. Pam stood there, quietly meditating and basking in his embrace.

Kenn Gulliksen

RESOURCES

Vineyard History
https://vineyardusa.org/about/history/

The Oasis of Hollywood
Judy Radachy, Founder
https://www.oasisofhollywood.org/internship/https://www.oasisofhollywood.org/about-oasis/history/

The Dream Center
Mathew and Carolyn Barnett
https://www.dreamcenter.org/

Teen Challenge
https://www.teenchallenge.org/centers/ministry-institute/

New Life Ministry
https://newlife.com

Lonnie Frisbee
http://lonnierayfrisbee.com

Keith Green
https://www.kevinhalloran.net/keith-green-story-movie/

The Second City
https://en.wikipedia.org/wiki/The_Second_City

The Second City has consistently been a notable starting point for comedians, award-winning actors, directors, and others in show business.

ENDNOTES

Chapter Three: Disillusioned Daze

[1] *Earlier in the year:* Joel Achenbach, "A Party That Had Lost Its Mind," Retropolis (August 24, 2018), https://www.washingtonpost.com/news/retropolis/wp/2018/08/24/a-party-that-had-lost-its-mind-in-1968-democrats-held-one-of-historys-most-disastrous-conventions/

[2] *Jerry Rubin summed it up:* Ibid.

Chapter Eleven: Heel Marks to the Cross

[3] *As iron sharpens:* Proverbs 27:17 NASB.

Chapter Thirteen: The Pain of Tarnished Souls

[4] *Teen Challenge program:* Teen Challenge is a ministry birthed by David Wilkerson on the streets of New York, a story told in the book and movie *The Cross and the Switchblade*. The one-year Biblical discipleship programs help teens and adults learn to live life free from life-controlling issues through the power of Jesus Christ. https://teenchallengeusa.org

Chapter Fifteen: Treasures in the Wilderness

[5] *Nothing is impossible:* Matthew 17:20.

[6] *Moses went to the desert:* Moses: Exodus 3:1; Jesus: Matthew 4:1; Paul: Galatians 1:17.

[7] *The goodness of the Lord:* Romans 2:4.

---

[8] *Abraham didn't have a clue:* Hebrews 11:8.

Chapter Sixteen: Mentors and Mercy

[9] *Handed her a Bataka:* "Learn to Handle Your Anger," JH-Products, https://jh-products.de/en/brands/batakas-encounter-bat/

[10] *Then you will know:* John 8:32.

[11] *words of knowledge:* A word of knowledge is a form of revelation similar to prophecy or a type of discernment, https://www.bible-knowledge.com/the-word-of-knowledge/

[12] *Where two or more gather:* Matthew 18:20.

[13] *Don't you think that anxiety:* tormentor—a person who inflicts severe mental or physical suffering on someone. Oxford University Press (2020), tormentor, in: lexico.com, available at: www.lexico.com/en/definition/tormentor.

[14] *The king said to him:* Matthew 18:34.

[15] *In this same way:* Matthew 18:35.

[16] *Do not despise:* Zechariah 4:10.

Chapter Seventeen: Grace Builders

[17] *Lanterman-Petris-Short Act:* Douglas Mossman, "*United States v Lyons:* Toward a New Conception of Legal Insanity," *The Journal of the American Academy of Psychiatry and the Law* (1988), http://jaapl.org/content/16/1/49.

[18] *weeping lasts...joy comes:* Psalm 30:5.

Chapter Eighteen: Brown Bag Healing

[19] *He has made everything beautiful:* Ecclesiastes 3:11.

Chapter Nineteen: Returning to Egypt

[20] *John Wimber:* "John Wimber," VineyardUSA, https://vineyardusa.org/about/john-wimber/

[21] *Lord, please! Send:* Exodus 4:13 NLT.

[22] *When the Son sets you free: Who You Say I Am, There Is More,* Hillsong Worship (2018). Paraphrase of John 8:36.

[23] *The things you have heard:* 2 Timothy 2:2.

[24] *apostolic anointing:* "Spiritual Gift of Apostleship," Spiritual Gifts Test, https://spiritualgiftstest.com/spiritual-gift-apostleship/

[25] *Lonnie Frisbee:* http://www.freedomcrusade.org/bio.

[26] *The Vineyard burst forth:* "History and Legacy," https://vineyardusa.org/about/history/

[27] *John Wimber:* "John Wimber," VineyardUSA, https://vineyardusa.org/about/john-wimber/

[28] *international Vineyard movement:* "Our Global Family," VineyardUSA, https://vineyardusa.org/about/our-global-family/

[29] *And since we are his children:* Romans 8:17 TLB.

Chapter Twenty: Doing It All Again

[30] *Friends, when life gets really difficult:* 1 Peter 4:12–13 MSG.

[31] *Seek first the kingdom:* my paraphrase of Matthew 6:33; Ephesians 3:20; 1 Corinthians 13:8.

[32] *Many are called:* Matthew 22:14 NLT.

Made in the USA
Monee, IL
11 July 2023

39031331R00118